in friendship,

Welter

Biblical Human Failures

Biblical Human Failures

Lot, Samson, Saul, Jonah, Judas

Walter Vogels

NOVALIS

© 2007 Novalis, Saint Paul University, Ottawa, Canada

Cover: modified images, Plaisted
Layout: Christiane Lemire

Business Offices:

Novalis Publishing Inc.
10 Lower Spadina Avenue, Suite 400
Toronto, Ontario, Canada
M5V 2Z2

Novalis Publishing Inc.
4475 Frontenac Street
Montréal, Québec, Canada
H2H 2S2

Phone: 1-800-387-7164
Fax: 1-800-204-4140
E-mail: books@novalis.ca
www.novalis.ca

Library and Archives Canada Cataloguing in Publication

Vogels, Walter, 1932–
    Biblical human failures : Lot, Samson, Saul, Jonah, Judas / Walter Vogels.

Includes bibliographical references.
ISBN-13: 978-2-89507-837-1
ISBN-10: 2-89507-837-8

    1. Failure (Psychology)--Biblical teaching. 2. Failure (Psychology)–
Religious aspects–Christianity. 3. Bible–Biography. I. Title.

BS571.V63 2007   220.9'2   C2006-906152-1

Scripture quotations taken from the Jerusalem Bible, published and copyright © 1966, 1967 and 1968 by Darton, Longman & Todd, Ltd and Doubleday, a division of Random House, Inc.

Printed in Canada.

We acknowledge the financial support of the Government of Canada through the Book Publishing Industry Development Program (BPIDP) for our publishing activities.

5   4   3   2   1   11   10   09   08   07

Contents

Introduction

The Bible has inspired people for many centuries. It is remarkable that it continues to touch the lives of people belonging to a variety of cultures in even the most distant parts of the globe. It has been translated into hundreds of languages, and there is often more than one translation available for the same language group. The number of English translations is impressive, and these translations are updated frequently. We have, for instance, The New American Bible, The New American Standard Bible, The New English Bible, The New International Version, The New Jerusalem Bible, The New King James Version, The New Life Version, The New Living Translation and The New Revised Standard Version. The Bible has also been commented upon in books and articles and on websites. The number of studies is beyond imagination: no one, not even scholars who dedicate their whole lives to the study of the Bible, could even dream of reading everything that is available. Whether they are academic, spiritual or pastoral, these studies prove that people continue to attach much importance to this unique piece of literature. It seems that there is no end to the new insights that this Book continues to inspire in its readers; it is like a well that never runs dry.

The Bible is not one book, but a collection of books. In a sense it is a library of books that are very different from each other. We can classify them into two broad categories. First, many books seem to be *didactic* – a form of teaching or instruction. For instance, the Prophetic Books do not reveal much about the private life of these great preachers, but they contain the message of these men of God: their preaching. The Wisdom Books do not tell us much about these sages or about their schools, but they contain their observations on life based upon their experience, expressed in proverbs, in instructions or in reflections, some of which are very critical. The collections of laws we find in the Torah (or Pentateuch) also belong to that type of literature. These laws are guidelines for human behaviour. We could, therefore, look at the Bible and try to figure out what that Book is teaching us about and for life, how we could or should live. I tried to sum up the biblical teaching in a previous book, *Becoming Fully Human: Living the Bible with God, Each Other and the Environment* (Novalis, 2003). There I suggested that the whole biblical teaching could be summarized by saying that the Bible presents us humans as living in relationship. More precisely, we are determined by a triple relationship: our relationship with God, with others and with nature. The Bible contains important teachings and principles on these three relationships that really can make us better and more complete human beings in our modern world, where other values often dominate.

But the Bible contains a second category of literature: *narrative*. The Bible is full of stories! Of course, through stories the writer is also teaching, but it is a more subtle way of doing so and perhaps, therefore, a more appealing one. Down through the ages, people all over the world have shared their stories. It is not surprising, given our love of stories, that these biblical stories continue to captivate readers. Many of the so-called children's bibles concentrate on that aspect. But stories appeal not only to children. Adults, including modern, more technical, trained readers still enjoy that type of literature, especially if these stories are well written and contain some suspense. We find these biblical stories mostly in the Pentateuch (Torah) and in the Historical Books (called the Earlier Prophets in the Hebrew tradition).

What makes a story? Every story needs characters and a plot. The narrative texts of the Bible are not necessarily historical; they may be fables, parables or myth. Some of the most beautiful stories in the Bible are found in the prehistory (Genesis 1–11). While these are perhaps the best known, they are often the most misunderstood. Anyone who has even an elementary knowledge of the Bible is familiar with the stories of Adam and Eve, Cain and Abel, Noah and the flood, and the building of the Tower of Babel, which ends in the confusing of the languages. A study of these apparently simple stories can reveal the rich message of these texts that can tell us so much about who we are as human beings.[1] After all, stories are not intended only to entertain, but also to instruct.

The prehistory speaks about humanity, not about Israel. But after these first eleven chapters of Genesis, the Bible includes stories about the ancestors of Israel and about the Israelites themselves. These stories do not belong to one literary genre. They are not all "historical" – and certainly not in the way we understand that word today. Often there is a mixture of historical and legendary elements, like the stories we tell about the founders of our tribes or nations and about our national heroes. Besides, these biblical stories are always religious history: God, as well as human actors, often plays an active role in them.

The list of all the biblical characters, men and women of Israel, would be very long, not to mention the many foreigners, Israel's enemies or friends, who also appear in these stories. Books and articles have been written on many of these characters. A few of them, however, are more central figures – because of their importance in the history of Israel, because of the length of the texts consecrated to them, and because of the role they continue to play in the later Jewish, Christian and, sometimes, Muslim traditions. Three figures stand out as perhaps the greatest. The texts sing their praises, without covering up their shortcomings and mistakes; in fact, they are described at times in startlingly honest terms.

The first is Abraham, the patriarch. An entire section of the book of Genesis is consecrated to him (Genesis [11:27-32] 12:1–25:11). The text describes how this man followed God's call, making it possible for God to start the restoration of his plan of salvation, which would affect not only Israel but also humanity as a whole. Abraham was heroic in his faith to accept his call, to trust in God's promises although they seemed humanly impossible. He was even ready to sacrifice his son, Isaac. It comes as no surprise that he is considered "the father of believers." But this exemplary person is also a weak person; he has no scruples about endangering his wife Sarah to save his own life – twice (Genesis 12:10-20; 20:1-18).

The second important biblical character is Moses, the central figure of four books of the Bible (Exodus, Leviticus, Numbers and Deuteronomy). Moses freed his people from slavery in Egypt, and then gave Israel its organization through the covenant and the law. He is the founder of a people and is said to have been the greatest prophet ever. The whole Torah (Pentateuch – the first five books of the Bible) has been attributed to him. And yet, he too is presented as very human, with his negative side. Even though he freed his people and led them to the Promised Land, he could never enter into that land himself; as punishment for his sin, he only enjoyed a glance of it before he died. The biblical text describes it rather mysteriously, but one thing is clear: Moses had lacked faith (Numbers 20:1-13).

The third person who played a central role in the history of Israel is David. His story also covers many chapters in the Bible (1 Samuel 16:1 – 1 Kings 2:11). David succeeded in building a united kingdom between all the tribes, between the North and the South; he made Jerusalem the political capital and the religious centre. Because he can be called the founder of the kingdom and of the nation of Israel, he entered history as the great king. Even most of the psalms are attributed to him. But once again, with all the admiration the Bible has for him, it does not hide his at times reprehensible conduct. He commits adultery with Bathsheba, and when she becomes pregnant, he gives orders to make sure that her husband, Uriah, gets killed in the war (2 Samuel 11) in order to cover up his own behaviour. From that moment on, David is miserable. The king has no more control over the situation, not even over the sexual misconduct and violence in his own family (2 Samuel 9 – 1 Kings 2).

The fact that the Bible presents its great men as they are, with their good and bad sides, makes them more attractive. They are real, great and weak, and thus human like us. For this reason, we can identify with them more easily than with some of the saints, whose lives are so out of the ordinary, admirable but hard to imitate. It is thus understandable that these three great biblical men continued to play an important role in the later tradition; they are, of all the Old Testament characters, the most quoted in the New Testament. But Abraham, Moses and David do not exhaust the great figures of the Old Testament; there are many more, including Jacob, Joseph, King Solomon, and others. At the sides of these great men we find great women. The story of Abraham cannot be understood without Sarah,[2] for example. But these women often play a secondary role. Some women, however, play a primary role, and certain women, such as Ruth and Esther, even have a book consecrated to them. Many of these men and women have been studied by scholars and have inspired readers. We could add the prophets to the list of great men. In the Historical Books (the earlier prophets in the Hebrew tradition) we find the stories of Samuel,

Elijah and Elisha, who have been studied in monographs. The Prophetic Books, however, provide very few stories. These contain the preaching of the classical prophets but not much of their biographies – with a few exceptions, such as the marriage story of the prophet Hosea (Hosea 1–3).[3] I limit myself here to the Old Testament; if I were to include the New Testament, then the person of Jesus would beat all other biblical characters in terms of the number of articles and books written.

What these biblical figures, especially the three great men of the Old Testament – Abraham, Moses and David – have in common is that theirs are success stories. They are people who made it! Studying each of these heroes teaches us a lot about them, and about human nature.[4]

But besides these stories of people who made it, we find many stories of those who did not make it. These are the biblical stories of human failure. Hagar,[5] the Egyptian slave-girl who gave Sarah and Abraham a child, was brutally expelled into the desert. Hagar did not really make it! The same can be said about Ishmael, Hagar's son, who was no longer needed or wanted once Isaac was born (Genesis 16:1-16; 21:8-21). Joab was the cruel military leader whom David wanted to put aside but was not able to, and then gave his son Solomon the task of eliminating Joab (1 Kings 2:5, 28-35). The priest Abiathar served under David but was expelled by Solomon from Jerusalem to Anathoth, which deprived him and his family of the priesthood (1 Kings 2:26-27). For whatever reason, just or unjust, these are just a few of the people who did not make it.

In this book, I look at a few of the more representative of such human failures covering the different periods of the history of Israel. In the period of the patriarchs we meet Lot, a failed patriarch. In the troubled period of the Judges, we find Samson, a failed judge. When, after this difficult period, Israel introduced the monarchy, there is Saul, a failed king. In the period of the monarchy parallel to the kings,

God sends a number of prophets. One of them, Jonah, was a failed prophet. These four figures cover some of the more important political and religious functions in Israel. Even if this book is first of all consecrated to the Old Testament, the New Testament also contains stories of people who made it and people who didn't. I include in this volume, then, the tragic character of Judas, a failed apostle. I study these five men together in one volume because I want to present a kind of synthesis, and because the texts in which they are described are generally not that long and my analysis does not intend to be technical or exhaustive.

Texts are never indifferent or neutral. They are always written from a certain perspective. Likewise, readers are never neutral; they also read from their perspective. Books of history support the winners; the losers are dead and cannot defend themselves. If the losers ever wrote their story, these tend to disappear. It is obvious that some sections of the story of David, especially his ascension to the throne, represent an anti-Saul and a pro-David viewpoint, while others, especially the succession story, has a pro-Solomon one. The Bible is full of conflicts between prophets. An interesting case is the famous dispute between Jeremiah and Hananiah (Jeremiah 28). They are both called "prophet"; they fight each other, insult each other and condemn each other. But we have only the text of Jeremiah, because he is the prophet who made it, while Hananiah did not make it. We might have a very different insight if we had Hananiah's text to reveal his side of the conflict. The gospels make it clear that Judas is a failed apostle, but it would have been much more revealing if Judas had left us his interpretation of the gospel story. Alas, we do not have the writings of the losers or of the failed characters.

This, however, is no obstacle for the purpose of this book. My intention is not to figure out the precise historical events and facts, or to discover the psychology of these five characters. I do not intend to make a judgment or condemn them. On the contrary, they merit a lot of respect, sympathy and compassion. In my approach to these human failures, I take the biblical text as it is, in its final form. This final form is the canonical text, which means the normative text. I want to find out why, in the eyes of the writer of the text, each person is presented as a failed character.

As we have said, stories are written to entertain but also to teach. The success stories do precisely that. They are exciting to read and teach us a lot about human behaviour. The same is true of be the stories of human failure. They may not always make us laugh, although sometimes they do, and at other times they make us nearly weep. They can be humorous or ironic, but also dramatic or tragic. They also teach. They tell us why these people failed. We could say that the stories of human failure teach us negatively what the success stories say positively. Just as the success stories do not only praise their heroes, but often describe in detail their stupidities and faults, so also the stories of human failure do not present only the shortcomings of their heroes or victims; they do not hesitate to stress their good sides. No one is totally exalted or totally rejected. Each human person is a mixture of greatness and of weakness. The difference lies in which of the two is the dominating factor in the person. The question, of course, is "why?" These texts may us help to discover the answer – or at least the beginning of it – so we can solve the mystery of human behaviour and of human failure.

I will follow the same approach for each of the five characters I examine. The first part consists of some brief critical introductory observations concerning the texts; the second part, which is the longer and more important, presents a close reading of the story itself; the third and final part is a theological conclusion that summarizes why, according to the story, that person failed.

May these stories entertain and teach you on your journey through the Bible!

1

LOT: *A Failed Patriarch*
(Genesis 11:27–19:38)

Critical Observations

Lot appears regularly in the book of Genesis and, more precisely, in the story of Abraham. He is mentioned for the first time in 11:27; the last reference to him – or, rather, to his family – is in 19:38. We have, therefore, the beginning and the end of Lot's story, even if he does not appear in all the chapters in between. It is significant that all the studies of this section of the Bible speak about the "Abraham-cycle" ([11:27–32] 12:1–25:11) and nobody ever speaks about the "Lot-cycle" (11:27–19:38).[6] Already we can see an interesting difference between the winner and the loser.

In the Abraham-cycle (the chapters whose main actor is Abraham), the mysterious character of Lot appears and reappears constantly. This material is complex. First of all, the story of Abraham could easily have been told without Lot. Some scholars, therefore, believe that the texts related to Lot came from a different source. Not only that: some scholars see a contradiction in how Lot is presented. Once he appears to be a rich shepherd with plenty of flocks (ch. 13), but on another occasion he is a city dweller (ch. 19). This discrepancy led historical critics to propose different layers, sources and traditions in these texts. While this may be a valid approach, we can see a beautiful harmony between all the texts related to the person of Lot. In many ways, the Lot-cycle fits perfectly inside the Abraham-cycle.

We touch here on the difference in today's biblical studies between *diachronic* and *synchronic* approaches. As I indicated in the introduction, I take the final, canonical form of the text, and that canonical text makes perfect sense.

The literary genre of the texts of the Lot-cycle is exactly the same as that of the Abraham-cycle, which is obviously a legend. This does not mean that there is no historical value whatsoever in the Abraham stories, or that Abraham could not be an historical person, but these texts are clearly full of legendary elements. Any reader can see that this genre applies equally to the stories of Lot. The best-known story of the Lot-cycle is probably the one about his wife. Contrary to God's command, she looks back at the city they just left and she turns into a pillar of salt (19:26). Such a story belongs to popular legends explaining some shapes of the rocks in the region of the Dead Sea, where the salt is everywhere. Fervent guides even today show the so-called wife of Lot.

If the narrator of these texts puts Lot continually beside Abraham, we can at least suspect that he may be comparing or opposing these two characters. And since there is no doubt that for him Abraham is the hero, we may then conclude that Lot is not his hero. The narrator may be trying to prove his thesis once positively in Abraham, and then once negatively in Lot.

Stories are always told from a particular perspective. Since the biblical writer is an Israelite, he looks at things from an Israelite perspective; after all, Abraham is Israel's ancestor. As often happens, when people speak about their neighbours they may become very critical, even negative and hostile. This is clearly visible at least in the story that explains the origin of Moab and Ammon, two peoples of Transjordan (19:30-38). The story is pro-Israel but anti-Moab and anti-Ammon. However, we can still see what the narrator reproaches these two peoples for, and what he sees as a difference between them and Israel, and, consequently, between Abraham the ancestor of Israel and Lot the ancestor of Moab and Ammon.

There must have been many stories about Abraham, the first patriarch. The final redactor has chosen some stories and left out others, and has put them in a particular order. He has given a beautiful unity to the various traditions concerning Abraham by grouping everything around the theme of the divine promises: the promise of a blessing, the promise of descendants and the promise of the land. All the texts of the Abraham-cycle are centred round these promises. God gives the promises, repeats them and confirms them, while Abraham responds to them in various ways: he believes, doubts or hesitates. The person of Lot must then also illustrate somehow, in his own way, something related to these three promises.

The Story of Lot

A close reading of the Lot story shows clearly that Lot is nearly always mentioned in parallel, and often in contrast, with Abraham.

Both their stories begin with a genealogy (11:27-32). "These are Terah's descendants: Terah became the father of Abram, Nahor and Haran. Haran became the father of Lot" (v. 27). Abraham[7] is listed as the eldest son of the family; he must have enjoyed all the privileges attached to that status. The text adds immediately that Haran, the youngest of Terah's three sons, also had a son, who was Lot. It is strange that the narrator starts with the third son, while the information that his second son, Nahor, also became a father and of two sons is mentioned only a few verses later (v. 29). The narrator, by presenting the genealogy this way, puts Lot, right from the beginning of the story, very close to Abraham. Lot is somehow placed ahead in the family, but it is also clear that he belongs to the next generation. With all the respect attached to age in those days, Abraham has another privileged position. But of course that is just how life goes, and such circumstances are beyond our control.

Abraham and Lot have at least one thing in common. The narrator uses exactly the same formula to speak about their birth: "Terah became the father of Abram" and "Haran became the father of Lot." This is the regular way to speak about a normal, natural birth. There is nothing extraordinary, nothing marvellous about it; neither of the two is the fruit of a special divine promise or intervention, something we find for other biblical characters, such as Ishmael, Isaac, Samson, Samuel and Jesus.

The narrator adds another piece of information: "Haran died in the presence of his father Terah in his native land, Ur of the Chaldaeans" (v. 28). The fact that he places the death of Haran even before mentioning the marriage of Abraham and Nahor (v. 29), suggests that Haran must have died early, and consequently Lot must have lost his father while he was still young. He is somehow an orphan, which obviously must have had serious consequences for him. He had a sad experience early in life. Abraham also lost his father but much later in life, since Terah lived "two hundred and five years" (v. 32).

One day the patriarch Terah decided to migrate: "Terah took his son Abram, his grandson Lot the son of Haran, and his daughter-in-law the wife of Abram, and made them leave Ur of the Chaldaeans to go to the land of Canaan. But on arrival in Haran they settled there" (v. 31). Terah does not take with him his second son and his family, and no reason is given for that. Nahor, therefore, must have stayed behind in Ur. Terah only takes Abram and the son of Haran. The way the text lists the actors is significant. One would have expected first Abraham and then his wife and only then in third position the grandson Lot. By naming the actors as he does, the narrator puts Abraham and Lot side by side, but stressing again that they belong to two different generations: one is a son, the other is a grandson. And yet, they again have something in common: neither chooses his own destiny. The patriarch Terah makes that decision for them; he "took" them on this journey, and their advice is not asked for.

It is only in the next story (12:1-9) that a major difference appears between Abraham and Lot. "The LORD said to Abram, 'Leave… So Abram left as the LORD told him" (vv. 1, 4).[8] His father is dead and now Abraham takes his life in his own hands, but his decision is very particular. He decides about his future in a response to a divine call. There, where he had followed his father from Ur to Haran, he now follows God, leaving Haran to go to the land of Canaan. The LORD, besides calling Abraham, also offers him three promises: a blessing, descendants and land. These promises are all very appealing, which could explain why Abraham accepts, but at the same time they seem rather unreal at this point. How can Abraham expect to have descendants if he is already 75 years old (v. 4) and his wife Sarah is barren (11:30)? How can he expect to receive the land since the Canaanites are now in that land (v. 6)? But somehow, Abraham trusts God, and without any further questions or objections, he goes.

At this important moment in the life of Abraham, Lot also has a decision to make. He has at least three options. First, he could decide to return to Ur of the Chaldaeans, if he felt that Terah had forced him to leave his homeland. He would have found there his uncle Nahor and his family who had not moved to Haran. Second, he could stay where he was, in Haran. By now Lot was no longer a young orphan; he had grown up and could go his own way. Third, he could go with his other uncle, Abraham. And that is what he decided to do: "and Lot went with him" (v. 4). We can make all kinds of hypotheses from this statement. Was Lot afraid to stay behind alone? Did he see some material advantages in following Abraham? Had he become so attached to Abraham that he considered him nearly as his father? Or did he perhaps feel that Abraham needed his help? Abraham, at 75, was indeed getting on in age. The list of suppositions could become very long. We could suggest many reasons, charitable or selfish. But we don't know, since the text does not expand on this, which means that the answer to that question is not important for the story. The only answer to the question of why Lot went with Abraham is that the narrator says so. And he does this because he wants to keep these two actors side by side to prove his thesis. After saying that Lot "went with him," the text adds another detail: "Abram took his wife Sarai, his nephew Lot, all the possessions…" (v. 5). Not only has Lot decided to go with his uncle, but Abraham accepts him. After all, Abraham could have refused. We could search again for reasons – selfish or charitable – why Abraham takes Lot with him, but the text does not expand on this either, and so this detail is unimportant. Note, however, the change in sequence for the actors. Here Sarah is mentioned before Lot, while earlier Lot came before Sarah (11:31). Abraham and Lot together leave Haran to go to Canaan.

The narrator has kept them side by side, but he has also introduced an important difference. Abraham leaves Haran in response to a divine call: he puts his trust in God; he does "as the Lord told him." And from now on, the story repeats often that God spoke or appeared to Abraham (see v. 7). God leads the life of Abraham, who responds. Lot also leaves Haran, but by a pure human decision: "he went with." The expression indicates following in the steps of someone else. Enoch and Noah walked "with" God (Genesis 5:22; 6:9). Lot follows Abraham, another human person; the story repeats that expression "with him" on other occasions. The text clearly shows the basic difference between the two men. The starting point in that period of their lives is very different, which determines the further development of their lives. Abraham puts himself under the guidance of God; Lot's life is a sequence of human decisions.

They are now both on the road to Canaan. The Lord appears and continues to speak to Abraham. In response, he builds altars to the Lord and invokes the name of the Lord (vv. 7-9). Nothing of this kind is said about Lot.

But famine hits the land. Lot may already have regretted choosing to go with Abraham. To find food, Abraham decides to go down to Egypt, where he behaves in a most scandalous way, endangering the life and honour of Sarah and bringing plagues on the king of Egypt. Pharaoh then expels him from that country. That story never refers to Lot, but, as we will see, he must have gone to Egypt too, which we can guess because he went "with" Abraham (12:10-20).

After their expulsion they return to Canaan. In this story, the narrator develops in much greater depth the contrast between Abraham and Lot (13:1-18). "From Egypt Abram returned to the Negeb with his wife and all he possessed, and Lot with him" (v. 1). The text thus indicates, indirectly, that Lot must have gone down to Egypt "with" Abraham. Note another small but significant change in the sequence of the actors here. When Abraham left Haran, the text says: "Abraham took his wife Sarai, his nephew Lot, all the possessions…" (12:5). On their return from Egypt, Sarah is still in first position, but even the possessions get priority over Lot, who is now in third position. The narrator keeps Lot together with Abraham, but at the same time he gradually puts Lot more and more at a distance. Lot started first before Sarah (11:31), then after Sarah but before the possessions (12:5), and now is after both her and the possessions (v. 1). Abraham has recognized in all these events the hand of God. He "invokes the name of the Lord" (v. 4), as he had done in the past. His life continues to be a dialogue with God even after his scandalous conduct in Egypt. Nothing of that kind of religious behaviour is said about Lot, "who was travelling with Abram" (v. 5). Simply, in these first verses, the text repeats that Lot is the man who goes "with" (vv. 1, 5).

The story of the return from Egypt reaches a turning point in the Abraham- and in the Lot-cycles. The beginning of that story still places the two actors in a remarkable parallel. Abraham comes back a rich man "with livestock" (v. 2), and so does Lot. He, too, has "flocks and cattle of his own" (v. 5). This, however, leads to a problem: "Dispute broke out between the herdsmen of Abraham's livestock and those of Lot's" (v. 7). Indeed, how can they all survive in a region where water is so scarce and where there is not much food to be found for these numerous animals? A common way that people solve such a problem is very simple: one kills the other, just as Cain killed his brother, Abel. But Abraham opts for another solution. He says to Lot: "Let there be no dispute between me and you…for we are brothers. Is not the whole land open before you? Part company with me: if you take the left, I will go right; if you take the right, I will go left" (vv. 8-9).

Abraham takes the initiative; he is the elder, and he makes this very clear. He puts himself first: "no dispute between me and you": he could have said between "you" and "me," which would perhaps have been more polite. But Abraham apparently wants to show that he is in control. He decides for a separation: "Part company with me." As we have noticed, the narrator has been putting more and more distance between Abraham and Lot as the story unfolds; Abraham completes this action by his order for a peaceful separation.

Why does Abraham choose this solution? Once again, many have speculated, for we have reached another gap in the text. Many readers stress the generosity of Abraham. He was the elder and the promise of the land was given to him. He could have claimed the whole land for himself, or at least made the first choice. Or Abraham could simply have expelled Lot; after all, Abraham had been good to him long enough. But then, one could also suggest that Abraham is afraid of Lot. Abraham was getting older, and thus weaker and weaker, while Lot must have been getting stronger and stronger. Abraham would have no chance in a fight between the two. It could thus very well be that Abraham acts to save at least part of the land for himself instead of risking losing everything. In any case, Lot does not make any objections or counterproposals. He goes along with the imposed solution, and he grasps the chance to make the first choice.

We could speculate on his reasons as well. Were Abraham's and Lot's reasons selfish or generous? But since the text does not specify their reasons, then that is not what is important in the story. The issue is the fact that Abraham and Lot, who had been together until now, are going to separate. This physical separation between the two, imposed by Abraham, will reveal the deep spiritual separation between them. What's more, it will reveal the spiritual contrast between them. This becomes extremely clear when we compare their different attitudes expressed in the two following paragraphs.

The first paragraph illustrates Lot's action (vv. 10-13). "Looking round, Lot saw all the Jordan plain, irrigated everywhere like the garden of the LORD or the land of Egypt, as far as Zoar." The text contains two verbs, "looking" and "seeing," and twice the idea of "all" and "everywhere." Everything Lot sees is "irrigated." The lack of water had been precisely the problem; there was not enough for both of them together, but now he is safe and his flocks are, too. What he sees is, to his great surprise, like "the garden of the LORD." Indeed, the Garden of Eden was well irrigated by four of the biggest streams of the world (Genesis 2:9-14). Lot sees paradise within his reach. And so he "chose all the Jordan plain for himself" – once more, we find the word "all" – and the text stresses clearly that he wants it for "himself." He consequently "moved eastwards." The reference to the paradise story is not limited to the "garden of the LORD." Lot's actions can be compared to the actions of the woman of the paradise story: "the woman saw...and that it was desirable... she took..." (Genesis 3:6). All seems fine and beautiful; nothing can go wrong. But the narrator tells the reader a detail that Lot does not know or even suspect: "this was before the LORD destroyed Sodom and Gomorrah." Lot, unknowingly, has made the wrong choice; he is doomed to lose everything. He should have remembered that the garden of the LORD was no longer accessible to humanity (Genesis 3:23-24).

The separation between Lot and Abraham is completed: "Thus they parted company." "Abraham settled in the land of Canaan," which is the Promised Land (12:6-7). Was Lot not aware that Canaan was the Promised Land? Whether he knew or not, Lot, consciously or unconsciously, puts himself outside the promise. And "Lot settled among the towns of the plain, pitching his tents on the outskirts of Sodom." To that statement the narrator adds another detail: "Now the people of Sodom were very vicious men, great sinners against the LORD." Lot, again, consciously or unconsciously, settles close to sin. And that also will lead to personal disaster.

The second paragraph returns to Abraham. Here the contrast with the first paragraph, related to Lot's choice, is remarkable (vv. 14-18). Lot had taken the initiative himself; here the LORD invites Abraham: "the LORD said to Abram." The text repeats the same verbs that are used for Lot. Abraham is asked by God to "look" around and to "see"; the text also, in several ways, stresses the idea of everything: "north – south; east – west" and "all the land." But now, and here is the big difference, while Lot "chose all for himself," God tells Abraham, "all the land I will give to you," and God goes on to say "and to you and your descendants for ever." Where the narrator has insinuated that everything Lot has chosen will be destroyed, we hear that what God gives to Abraham will be forever. And while Lot pitched his tents close to sin, Abraham's move implies something different: "so Abram went with his tents to settle at the Oak of Mamre, at Hebron, and there he built an altar to the LORD." One is close to sin; the other is close to the LORD.

Abraham and Lot are indeed separated – not only physically, but also spiritually. The narrator could not have shown a deeper contrast between the two. He had already illustrated the difference in their departure from Haran, where Abraham left as a response to a divine call and Lot left by a purely human decision. This contrast is confirmed in the story of their separation. Abraham is presented as the person who trusts God, and even if he took the risk of losing the better part by leaving the first choice to Lot, he will end up the winner. Lot is the person who bases his life upon his own initiative, who thinks to make the right choices. Lot has been attracted by wealth and he lives close to sin. That is why he will be twice a loser: once because of humans, once because of God. In both situations, even if both men now live separate lives, Abraham will still intervene in Lot's favour. At times the narrator continues to compare the two, who now live separate from each other, by viewing them in parallel or in contrast.

Lot had been attracted to the Jordan plain because of its richness and wealth. It does not, then, come as a surprise that others, too, envied that area. This leads to the first world war of four kings coming from the East against the five kings of that region, among them the kings of Sodom and Gomorrah (14:1-24). "The conquerors seized all the possessions of Sodom and Gomorrah, and all their provisions, and made off. They also took Lot, the nephew of Abram, and his possessions and made off; he was living at Sodom" (vv. 11-12). It did not take long for Lot to realize that he had made the wrong choice. This is the first time that Lot becomes the loser. He has not only lost what he owns, but also his own freedom.

Suddenly Abraham reappears in this war story:"Abram heard that his brother had been taken captive" (v. 14). They had gone their separate ways, but Abraham, instead of harbouring bad feelings towards Lot who, after all, had taken the better part, decides to intervene and to save Lot. Abraham had indeed been chosen by the LORD to become a blessing for others (12:2-3)."He recaptured all the goods, along with his brother Lot and his possessions…" (v. 16). The reader could again start trying to figure out why Abraham did this, but one thing is certain: he did not do it for selfish reasons. Lot had been attracted by the wealth of that region, and so were these four kings; the same cannot be said for Abraham, who states explicitly:"nothing will I take of what is yours; you shall not say,'I enriched Abram'. For myself, nothing" (vv. 23-24).

This short encounter between Abraham and Lot does not last long; they soon return to their own lives and choices. The following stories (15–18) speak only of Abraham without Lot. Then Lot reappears on his own, where we find him once more in Sodom, to which he must have returned (19:1-29). Obviously, Lot is attached to that place. But now he is going to lose everything a second time – not through the greed of humans this time, but through divine punishment, since Sodom is not only the place of wealth but also of sin.

Abraham receives three mysterious visitors who promise him the birth of his son, but who also inform him that the LORD is going to destroy Sodom because of the great sin of its citizens. Abraham pleaded with God to save the city if there were at least a certain number of just people.Two of the three messengers then go to Sodom and announce to Lot the divine decision concerning that place. In this section, the narrator continues to put Abraham and Lot, the two main actors, in parallel, even if they are no longer physically together. There is a beautiful symmetry and similarity between the visit of the messengers to Abraham (18:1-8) and the one to Lot (19:1-3).[9]

Abraham is the first to receive mysterious visitors: "The LORD appeared to him at the Oak of Mamre while he was sitting by the entrance of the tent during the hottest part of the day" (18:1). The narrator says that this visitor is "the LORD," but this must not have been evident to Abraham, since what he sees are "three men." But still, he suspects something, since he speaks to them at times in the singular "my Lord" but at other times reverts to the plural. The text, however, makes it clear that it is indeed a visit from the LORD (18:1, 13, 17, 20). Of these three visitors at the beginning, "two men" leave for Sodom, while "the LORD" stays with Abraham (18:22; see also v. 16). Abraham is now very conscious of being in the presence of the LORD, and pleads with him to save Sodom (18:22-23). This prepares us for a difference between Abraham's visitors and Lot's. The LORD stayed behind with Abraham and only these "two men," whom the text now calls "two messengers" (many Bibles translate this as "two angels"), arrive in Sodom: "When the two messengers reached Sodom in the evening, Lot was sitting at the gate of Sodom" (19:1). Like everyone else, Lot sees in these two messengers only "men." And indeed, the text makes that difference clear; Abraham received the visit of the LORD, while Lot receives two men. It will take Lot some time to figure out that these two men are messengers of the LORD; they even have to reveal that point to him (v. 13).

Another difference is that the visitors have come to Abraham's tent, while they now come to Sodom where Lot just happens to sit at the gate of the town. In a sense, they do not seem to have come directly for him. We could say that Abraham received visitors, while Lot encountered passersby. Both, however, treat these strangers with the same respect. "As soon as [Abraham] saw them he ran ...to meet them, he bowed to the ground" (18:2), the narrator tells us. Lot does the same: "As soon as Lot saw them he rose to meet them and bowed to the ground" (v. 1). The parallel could not be stronger.

Abraham and Lot do not only show their visitors some respect; they also offer them hospitality. Abraham says: "My Lord, I beg you … do not pass your servant by… before going further." In the meantime, he promises that water will be brought to them so they can "wash their feet"; he also offers them a meal, "a little bread." The meal becomes, however, more luxurious; there is not only bread but also cream, milk and a tender calf. Many people have stressed the great hospitality of Abraham, and there is some truth in this, but it is easy for him to welcome visitors, when Sarah and the servant have to do all the work. Abraham only puts before his visitors what others have prepared. Sarah is not even welcome to be present (18:3-8).

The reception that Lot reserves for the passersby of Sodom is parallel, and in some ways superior, to that of Abraham. Lot shows here what a nice and kind person he is; after all, there must have been other people at the city gate, but it is Lot who makes the invitation. Like Abraham did, he entreats: "I beg you, my lords, please come down to your servant's house to stay the night…. Then in the morning you can continue your journey" (v. 2). Since the visitors arrived at Abraham's tent at noon, he invites them just for a short stay, while Lot sees these strangers arriving at a city in the evening. Where are they going to spend the night? Inviting people in for the night is certainly much more disruptive to a family. Exactly like Abraham, Lot invites them to wash their feet. The visitors, perhaps afraid to impose upon Lot, refuse, saying, "We can spend the night in the open street." And indeed, they could have done so, as countless travellers must do. But Lot insists; he knows perhaps that they may be in danger in the street at night. After all, Sodom is a city of sinners. "He pressed them so much that they went home with him and entered his house." Again, like Abraham, Lot offers them a meal. The meal is not as copious as the one offered by Abraham, but then, how could a city dweller have a calf? Lot offers them what he has: bread. But in that meal Lot shows himself a finer host than Abraham, for he himself does the work, rather than leaving it to his wife or servant: "He prepared a meal for them, baking unleavened bread" (vv. 2–3).

In terms of the hospitality offered to the visitors or the passersby, Lot is certainly as generous as Abraham, if not more so. The narrator presents a Lot who is respectful, giving, a fine person, no less than his hero Abraham. There is, however, a significant difference here: when Abraham addresses the three men standing before his tent, he greets them with "My Lord"; he recognizes in these visitors a divine intervention. Lot, on the other hand, sees in the two messengers ordinary human visitors, and says to them, "my lords." In this, Lot is no different from the townspeople, who also speak of the two men (v. 5).

But Lot in all his kindness, may have acted too quickly. After all, he is a foreigner in Sodom; although he had settled there, he was not really a native of that town. Does he have the right to bring other foreigners into Sodom, especially in the dark of night? Today we might wonder if Lot is not suspected of being an illegal immigrant smuggler. And so Lot, in all his generosity, gets into trouble – not with a few people, but with the whole city. "The house was surrounded by the men of the town, the men of Sodom both young and old, all the people without exception" (v. 4). It is now Lot who is indeed alone against the whole town. Their request is clear: "Where are the men who came to you tonight? Send them out to us so that we may know them" (v. 5). The people want to find out who the visitors are. What are they doing here? Are they enemies or even spies? This text has often been interpreted in a sexual sense: the townspeople want "to know" the visitors, to abuse them sexually. That is also a possibility.

And now Lot once more shows his true character. "Lot came out to them at the door, and…closed the door behind him" (v. 6). There he is, standing alone before the angry crowd. He even closes the door behind him so that the two men are safe inside. Risking his own life, he begs the people of Sodom to respect his guests. In order to placate them he offers them a counterproposal: "Listen, I have two daughters who are virgins. I am ready to send them out to you, to treat as it pleases you. But as for the men, do nothing to them, for they have come under the shadow of my roof" (v. 8). Lot is torn. He has taken the responsibility to protect his visitors – after all, he has invited them into his house, even insisting that they come there after they had first refused. How can he hand them over to the mob? But his proposal is rather upsetting, too, and not at all respectful of his two daughters. It is indeed shocking, and readers have been very critical of him for this. Indeed, he has no excuse. But then, when we recall that the text has so often compared Lot with Abraham, we realize that Lot does no worse than Abraham did. On the contrary, Lot deserves more consideration than the father of believers. Abraham, to save his own life, causes Sarah to be taken first into the harem of the king of Egypt and later into the harem of the king of Gerar (12:10-20; 20:1-18). What Abraham did with his wife, Lot now does with his daughters, but with an important difference. Unlike Abraham, Lot is not trying to save himself; his aim is to protect the lives of his two visitors.

His proposal does not at all satisfy the people of Sodom. In fact, they remind him that he is a foreigner and therefore does not have the right to tell them what they should or should not do. "Now we will treat you worse than them," they say, and they don't leave it at that. They move into action: "They forced Lot back and moved forward to break down the door" (v. 9). Suddenly Lot receives help from the two men he wanted to save at all cost: "But the men reached out, pulled Lot back into the house, and shut the door" (v. 10). The two men look after Lot's security, like the LORD did during the flood when "he closed the door (of the ark) behind Noah" (Genesis 7:16). These two men are not only strong, they also have a very special power: they strike all the people at the door with blindness.

The story could have been finished here, but it starts all over again. The text reveals that these two men were not just strangers passing by, but that they had come with a message. It contains good news and bad news. The good news is "Have you anyone else here? Your sons, your daughters and all your people in the town, take them out of the place." The reason he must do so is the bad news: "We are about to destroy this place, for there is a great outcry against them, and it has reached the LORD. And the LORD has sent us to destroy them" (vv. 12-13). Lot is told for the first time that these two are not ordinary humans, but messengers of God. Once, four foreign kings had come to destroy the city of Sodom. They had captured the wealth of the city and had also taken Lot and his family. Now God has decided to destroy the same city, but this time as a punishment for the sins of the people. But Lot and his family are given a chance to escape. Why they get that opportunity is clearly linked with Abraham's prayer (18:16-33), where he begged God not to destroy the just with the wicked, and to save the city if there were at least ten just people. But Lot, his wife, his two daughters and the two future sons-in-law together are only six. That only these six are allowed to escape from the destruction proves that Lot is a good person. He reminds us of Noah, the only just one among that sinful humankind who, with his family, is saved from the total destruction caused by the flood (Genesis 6:5–9:17).

Trusting two men who claim to be messengers of God is not easy. Abraham had struggled with this, too. Even when God spoke to him, he did not always trust God. At times he had his doubts; for example, he had laughed when he heard that he would have a son (17:17). Sarah, too, had laughed when these visitors, who are now with Lot, promised that she would become the mother of a child (18:9-15). Lot does not laugh at all. In his first reaction he is inclined to believe what the two men told him, and tries to convince his family that the men can be trusted. But he encounters resistance. The rest of the story shows how one family member after the other has trouble believing.

Lot speaks first to his future sons-in-law, the men who are to marry his daughters. They must have been natives of the town of Sodom. Since "all the men of Sodom ... without exception" (v. 4) had been shouting at Lot's door, they must have been there too, unless they were already inside the house. They were likely rather upset when Lot offered the crowd his two daughters. It must have been awkward for Lot to face them now, but he does. He is concerned about them and about his daughters' future. After all, he is not a bad father! The messengers had said: "Take them out of this place. We are about to destroy this place." Instead of taking them, Lot invites his future sons-in-law, saying, "Come, leave this place, for the LORD is about to destroy this town" (v. 14). Perhaps Lot is still conscious of his grandfather "taking" him from Ur to Haran, without asking for his opinion on the matter (11:31), and of the kings "taking" him by force from Sodom (14:12). Lot is respectful of his future sons-in-law; he gives them all the information they need but lets them decide for themselves. "But the sons-in-law thought he was joking" (v. 14). Abraham and Sarah had laughed; these two young men also laugh. They must have been wondering: How can this great wealthy city be destroyed? The builders of the town and of the tower of Babel likely wondered the same thing

(Genesis 11:1-9). But it does happen, and even happens frequently, that human mega-projects come to a halt.

So the future sons-in-law remain unconvinced, which means two less who can be saved; the number is down to four. By now it has become dawn and so the messengers insist, they "urged Lot." They make him feel that the situation has become more and more serious. They tell him: "Come, take your wife and these two daughters of yours, or you will be overwhelmed in the punishment of the town" (v. 15). Note that the messengers repeat the same verb: "take" what is left of your family, force them if necessary. Do not leave the choice to them. The messengers make their point more clearly, this time. Instead of saying that the city will be destroyed, they say that Lot's family will be overwhelmed in the disaster. The narrator again clearly indicates that what is going to happen is a punishment for the city; Lot and his family are the just who are offered salvation.

We have reached a critical point in the story. Lot seems to have believed what the two messengers are telling him, but when it comes to action, it is a different story. "And as he hesitated, the men took him by the hand, and his wife and his two daughters, because of the pity the LORD felt for him. They led him out and left him outside the town" (v. 16). The two future sons-in-law had been laughing, and now Lot "hesitates." Is it ever difficult to leave that city of Sodom! And since Lot does not appear to accept the invitation freely, and since he does not take his wife and daughters as the messengers had requested, they do it for him: they "took by the hand" Lot and the rest of the family, and "led" them out of the town. The messengers of the LORD do not leave them the choice anymore; they force Lot and his family to leave. The narrator explains this surprising behaviour of God by describing the pity the LORD felt for Lot. The text frequently suggests God's grace for Lot (vv. 16, 19, 21).

We have noticed that the stories of Abraham and Lot often compare the two characters; here we see another important difference between them. The LORD called Abraham in a few simple words: "Leave…," and without any hesitation "Abram left as the LORD told him" (12:1.4). Even when God told Abraham: "Take your son… go… you shall offer him as a burnt offering…," Abraham's unquestioning response is: "Rising early next morning Abraham…took…his son Isaac" (22:2-3). Note that Abraham is here asked to "take" a member of his family, but in this case it is to sacrifice his son. Abraham does not hesitate; nobody has to force him. On the contrary, early in the morning he takes his son, ready to lead him to his death. Lot, also at dawn, is asked to take his children, not to their death but to their last chance of survival, and still Lot hesitates.

The story is not over yet. Lot, who had hesitated and has to be forced to leave his beloved Sodom, does not give up that easily. Instead of running for his life after he has been brought out of the city, he has to be encouraged to do so. The messengers tell him: "Run for your life. Neither look behind you nor stop anywhere on the plain. Make for the hills if you would not be overwhelmed" (v. 17). It is becoming more and more urgent. Lot has to run fast, and for the same reason: not to be overwhelmed. Who now would not run fast to save his life? But Lot says, "No, I beg you, my Lord." Remember that when Lot spoke for the first time to the two men at the city gate, he said, "I beg you, my lords"; now he says "my Lord." And from now on the text no longer speaks in the plural of two messengers, but in the singular "he." Lot has finally recognized in these two men the Lord, just as Abraham had done nearly from the beginning when he saw his three visitors (18:3). God acts and speaks through mediators. This is now the first time in the whole Lot story that he prays to God, but it is a strange prayer.

Lot's prayer (vv. 18-20) is not at all simple praise or pure thanksgiving as one would expect from someone who has been saved from such a disaster. His prayer is an attempt to change the mind of God: "No, I beg you, my Lord." In the first part of his prayer, Lot thanks God for the favours he has received and sings God's praises. This appears, however, to be merely an attempt to please God in order to obtain what he wants: "Your servant has won your favour and you have shown great kindness to me in saving my life." In the second part of his prayer he formulates his objection: "But…." The messengers had instructed him to run to the hills not to be overwhelmed, yet Lot says: "But I could not reach the hills before this calamity overtook me, and death with it." He obviously does not trust God very much. If God asked Lot to run for safety to the hills, would God not hold back the destruction until Lot reached safety? Otherwise, God might as well have left Lot in Sodom. And then, in the third part of his prayer, Lot finally formulates his request: "The town over there is near enough to flee to, and is a little one. Let me make for that – is it not little? – and my life will be saved." Why does Lot ask for that favour? The reason he gives is that he fears he will not to reach the hills in time. If this is really the case, then it suggests a lack of trust in God. Could it be that Lot has a hidden agenda? The last time Lot chose a new home, he selected the region of the Jordan plain "as far as Zoar," and had settled close to Sodom (13:10-13). Even then, he had his eyes on Zoar. The king of that city had also been involved in the famous war by the four invaders (14:2). While Lot has to give up his beloved Sodom, he remains attached to another town: Zoar. God is not going to refuse that request, he says to himself, since that town is only a "little" one. It even sounds as if Lot is manipulating God. By praying to seek refuge there, he indirectly prays that this city will be saved.

The LORD accepts Lot's request: "I grant you this favour too, and will not destroy the town you speak of. Hurry, escape to it, for I can do nothing until you reach it" (v. 21). This answer reveals explicitly that God would never have started the destruction before Lot was safe. Lot demonstrated a clear lack of faith in God when he said in his earlier prayer that he would not reach the hills in time. God's answer indicates that not only Sodom but also Zoar are on the list of places to destroy because of human wickedness. That leads us to another interesting contrast between Abraham and Lot. Abraham, in a very long prayer, had been bargaining with God to save the town of Sodom for the just people who could have lived there. He had dared to bargain down to ten just people (18:16-33). Lot, on the other hand, prays to save the town of Zoar not for its habitants, but for himself so he could escape there. Why was Lot able to convince God to go beyond his justice, and why did Abraham not succeed at this?

The story is drawing to a close: "As the sun rose over the land and Lot entered Zoar…" (v. 23). It had all started at "dawn" (v. 15); things have gone fast, and Lot is now safe in Zoar, along with his wife and daughters. "The LORD rained on Sodom and Gomorrah brimstone and fire from the LORD. He overthrew these towns and the whole plain, with all the inhabitants of the towns, and everything that grew there" (vv. 24-25). What a difference from what Lot had first seen when he chose for himself that same region (13:10-13). Then it looked like the garden of the LORD; now it is total destruction. This is the second time that Lot realizes that he has made the wrong choice, but still he remains attached to that town of Zoar. How difficult it is to let go, as his wife reminds us by her actions. "The wife of Lot looked back, and was turned into a pillar of salt" (v. 26). The two sons-in-law got their chance to save their lives, but they did not believe and they disappeared in the disaster. Lot was urged to leave; when he hesitated, the visitors saved him by forcing him. Of all the inhabitants of Sodom, only four made it out in time. They were warned not to stop and not to look back. Still, Lot's wife looks back. Who knows, she may have thought. Perhaps God has not destroyed the city; perhaps we can turn back to our beloved Sodom. The wife is another person who does not believe, and without belief there can be no salvation. So close to being saved, the wife is another loser. That family of Lot's certainly is a peculiar one, as the rest of the story confirms.

The narrator concludes this tragic story of total destruction with a personal reflection: "Thus it was that when God destroyed the towns of the plain, he kept Abraham in mind and rescued Lot out of disaster when he overwhelmed the towns where Lot lived" (v. 29). We recall that Lot has been saved twice. The first time, during the war of the foreign kings who attacked Sodom and made him captive, Abraham came to his rescue. The second time, once again in Sodom, Lot is saved from that total destruction by God, but again thanks to Abraham's intercession. This was indeed part of the promises given to Abraham, that he would be a blessing for others (12:2-3; 18:18).

Suddenly, the story takes a surprising turn: "After leaving Zoar Lot settled in the hill country with his two daughters, for he dared not stay at Zoar. He made his home in a cave, himself and his two daughters" (v. 30). When Lot, after all his hesitation, had been forced out of the city of Sodom, God had told him to run and "to make it for the hills" (v. 17). Lot had then begged God to let him settle in the town of Zoar, for he feared he could not reach the hills in time. God had assured Lot that he would be safe in Zoar, yet now that everything is over, Lot leaves that town and moves to the hills.

Why did he change his mind? The narrator gives the reason: "for he dared not stay in Zoar." Lot is said to be afraid, but of what? Once again, we can go in all kind of directions. Is he afraid that God would also soon destroy the city of Zoar after all? That would not say much about Lot's trust in God's promise that Lot was safe in Zoar. Or is Lot afraid that God would get angry because Lot had asked God to change his mind? Maybe Lot does not want to stay in the town where his wife died in a rather dramatic way, because such memories are too painful. The only thing we know for sure is that Lot is afraid. First he was afraid he would not reach the hills, and now he is afraid to stay in the town. Obviously, Lot is someone whose life is full of anguish; he has seen and experienced too much. He is perhaps afraid of himself, or of others, or of God, or a mixture of all of these. He does not feel safe anywhere. He does not seem to know what he wants. He has become incoherent. He moves into the darkness of a cave, hidden, far from danger.

The last story concerning Lot happens in that cave and it is not a happy one. The Lot-cycle has no happy ending! The two daughters, who are living in the cave with their father, concoct a wicked plan (vv. 31-38). "The elder said to the younger, 'Our father is an old man, and there is not a man in the land to marry us in the way they do the world over'" (v. 31). These two young women had both lost their future husbands in the disaster of Sodom, and they understandably want to get married. Above all, they want children. They say that there are no men in the land, but even though "all the habitants of the towns" (v. 25) had disappeared, the town of Zoar and its inhabitants had been saved, and there must have been people outside of the towns. But still, this is the daughters' conviction. And here is their solution: "Come let us ply our father with wine and sleep with him. In this way we shall have children by our father" (v. 32). This story reminds us of a similar one: that of Noah, who, just saved from the flood, gets drunk, uncovers himself in the tent, and is there abused by one of his sons. At least the two other sons show respect to their father (Genesis 9:20-24); Lot is less lucky; both his daughters abuse their father after they have made him drunk. In doing so, the daughters do not show any respect for their father, and their aims are selfish. But we must remember that they may have lost all respect for their father when he offered them to the mob to protect the two visitors. Perhaps they are now taking their revenge.

The two daughters act upon their plan. "That night they made their father drunk, and the elder slept with her father though he was unaware of her coming to bed or of her leaving" (v. 33). The next day the younger daughter does the same, and again "he was unaware of her coming or of her leaving" (v. 35). Lot is no longer in control. He does not even know what is happening to him; he is used and abused by his own daughters, completely unaware. The two daughters become pregnant, and each of them gives birth to a son. The elder calls her son Moab, and the younger calls her son Ben-Ammi. These are the ancestors of the Moabites and the Ammonites. Although they are the descendants of Lot, he does not even know that he is their father.

The narrator has made a clear parallel, and in this case once more a contrast, between Abraham and Lot concerning their descendants. Abraham, who had no children, had tried two human solutions. He had first adopted his servant Eliezer (15:3), and then he had Ishmael by Hagar as a surrogate mother (16:15). But his real son, Isaac, was not the result of human solutions but the fruit of God's promise (21:2-3). Lot, meanwhile, has two daughters by his wife. But the stories about how the lineage of Abraham and of Lot will carry on are extremely different. The two stories start in an identical way: "By now Abraham was an old man…" (24:1); the daughters of Lot also said that their father was "an old man." Abraham decides that the time has come to find a wife for Isaac (24:1-67). The servant who is charged with this task doubts that it is going to work out: "perhaps…." But Abraham has complete confidence in God: "He [God] will now send his messenger ahead of you...." Indeed, the story repeats in several places that everyone sees and agrees that this is the work of God, that Rebecca is the woman God intends to become Isaac's wife. Abraham is in control; as we have seen, Lot is not at all in control. He is not even aware of what is happening to him. Abraham's grandchildren are the fruit of God's plan; Lot's grandchildren are the fruit of human solutions and planning.

A final significant difference between Abraham and Lot is the ending of their stories. After Abraham had lived for 175 years, he died at "a ripe age, an old man who had lived his full span of years; and he was gathered to his people. His sons Isaac and Ishmael buried him in the cave of Machpelah..." (25:7-9). Like Abraham, Lot is also "an old man"; and they both end up in a "cave": Abraham to be buried in it, Lot to live in it. There we find Lot for the last time; he is like a living dead man. The two sons of Abraham pay their respect to their father; the two daughters of Lot abuse their father. Abraham was "gathered to his people" and is buried in beside his wife Sarah (24:10). The story of Lot docs not even end with his death and funeral; he is not "gathered with his people." After all, who does Lot have left? His father died when Lot was a young boy, and his wife has become a pillar of salt. Lot's life never achieves closure; he hides from the world, full of fear.

Theological Conclusion

The story of Lot is a sad one. From early in his life, when he loses his father, he is not in control. Others make decisions for him: first his grandfather and then Abraham. They take him wherever they decide to go. At the end of the story, Lot again is not in control. His two daughters decide for him and abuse him.

In between these two moments, when Lot is free to make his own decisions, he always seems to make the wrong choices. He goes with Abraham to Canaan, but there the land is hit with famine. He chooses Sodom, thinking it the right thing to do, but twice he becomes the victim of this choice. Inviting passersby into his house nearly costs him his life. It becomes perhaps understandable that at a certain moment he does not know what to choose anymore. He is offered the hills. No, he wants the town. He is offered the town. No, he wants the hills.

Lot is not perfect. He seems to be attracted too much by material wealth, but who is not? Abraham, too, did not despise all the wealth he got in Egypt, for instance. Lot was not respectful to his daughters when he offered them to the angry crowd of Sodom to save the life of his visitors. But even in that behaviour he was better than Abraham, who offered his wife to others to save his own life. Lot is far from being a bad person. On the contrary, he is generous: hospitable and welcoming, even more than Abraham is. He may have been too generous, not thinking of all the consequences of bringing people into a town where he is an immigrant. In Lot, like in all human beings, there are the two sides: weakness and goodness. But without a doubt, Lot is a just person; otherwise, God would not have selected him to be saved from the destruction of Sodom. Lot is different from the sinful people of Sodom. As a human person he can stand the comparison with Abraham and has no reason to be ashamed.

But there is an essential difference between the two figures. The life of Abraham is a constant dialogue between him and God. The LORD calls Abraham, speaks to him and appears to him. Abraham recognizes the LORD, listens to him, prays to him, invokes him and builds altars for him. That does not mean that Abraham never has his doubts, never hesitates, even to the point of turning to human solutions. But Abraham and God always find each other again in their ongoing dialogue. The narrator has formulated it in a very strong statement: "Abram puts his faith in the LORD, who counted this as making him justified" (15:6). There lies the deep and fundamental difference with Lot. People have made decisions for Lot, and Lot has made decisions by himself, but there is no reference whatsoever to God. He never invokes the name of the LORD; he does not build altars for the LORD. Even after his liberation from the conquering kings, he has no word of thanks for God.

Of course, one could say that God did not call Lot when he called Abraham, or that God did not speak to Lot like he did to Abraham. But it may well be that Lot did not hear the voice of God because he did not listen. It did not take much time for Abraham to discover God in the three visitors, but Lot discovered that the two men were divine messengers only after they told him so. And when he learned that they came with a message from God, he did not trust them. Instead of accepting gratefully the chance they give him to be saved, he hesitates so much that they have to force him to freedom. Only then, for the first time in his life, did he realize that he was in the presence of God. In the middle of that tragic situation, Lot – for the first time and also for the last time, towards the end of his life – prays. Some people approach God only in hopeless situations. And that only prayer of Lot is far from being an acceptance of God's will: on the contrary, it is an attempt to change God's mind to fit his own plan.

The narrator has presented two fine people, humanly speaking, but who are different from each other on one important point. Abraham bases his life not only on his own decisions, but also, and primarily, on God. Abraham is therefore "the father of believers"; he is, in the eyes of the narrator, the successful patriarch. Lot, on the other hand, bases his life exclusively on his own decisions. He is therefore "the father of unbelievers"; in the eyes of the narrator, he is the failed patriarch.

2

SAMSON: A Failed Judge
(Judges 13–16)

Critical Observations

The Book of Judges contains a clearly defined section on Samson, another person who qualifies as a failed character in the biblical tradition. This section begins with a long text describing the marvellous announcement of Samson's birth and then the birth itself, followed by a series of his adventures. The story ends with his death and funeral. The parameters of Samson's story are straightforward and agreed upon by all scholars: it covers four chapters of the Book of Judges (13–16).[10]

The story is so strange, we wonder what its function could be in the Scriptures, which we proclaim to be the Word of God. While his birth is miraculous – Samson is a gift from God to his pious parents – he himself is rather different. He is a judge who sleeps with prostitutes, wreaks a tremendous violence in his personal revenge against the Philistines, and ultimately sacrifices himself in order to kill as many people as possible. Today we would call him a suicide bomber. The story is a sad mixture of sex, violence and religion. For this reason, biblical commentators do not have much good to say about this judge! But people in other fields rate Samson as more successful. Abusive sex and violence are topics that have to be condemned on the surface, but are often enjoyed in secret. And so, Samson has inspired many artists, writers, painters, composers and moviemakers. His girlfriend Delilah has certainly helped to make his story exciting and to nourish the imagination. Even many children's bibles reproduce stories and pictures of Samson, especially the one in which he makes the temple come tumbling down on the poor Philistines.

But the story of Samson, which seems to form a clear literary unit, also raises questions. The Book of Judges tells the stories of six major and six minor judges. This group of twelve is a significant number, since it corresponds to the twelve tribes of Israel. These judges are generally not what we think of as court judges, but rather military leaders who liberated Israel from the oppression of their enemies so that Israel could enjoy some peace and rest until the next enemy aggression. Samson's story, which comes at the end of the book, is markedly different from the stories of all the others. His violent exploits are not to help his people, but only to take personal revenge. It seems, then, that the story of Samson comes from another tradition and was added to the other stories. And, by the way, he is the thirteenth judge: an unlucky number.

How the Samson story ever entered into the Book of Judges can be questioned, but besides that, several scholars suggest that the origin of these four chapters is complex. They stress that the birth narrative (ch. 13) is very religious and in total contrast with the rest of the Samson story, which is profane and secular (ch. 14–16). They propose, therefore, a different source for these two blocks of texts. Some go even further, believing that in these three chapters, the few verses that refer to God (14:4a, 6, 19a; 15:14, 18ff; 16:17, 20, 28) were later additions, intended to give a religious colour to these profane texts when they were combined with the pious birth narrative. We also notice that the three chapters covering the adventures of Samson contain very similar stories. We could call them two cycles. Chapter 16 repeats in part what is told in chapters 14 and 15; and both these sections have a similar ending (15:20 and 16:31), which could suggest that they may have a different origin.

These observations are all valid and typical for the diachronic approach to texts in biblical studies. But the synchronic approach has also value and deserves attention, as we discovered in the Lot story. Whether the Samson story was a later addition to the Book of Judges does not really affect our study. These four chapters form a unit that has its place in the book, and this Samson story functions perfectly in itself. This is likely how the final editor or redactor wanted it. He must have had a special intention by mixing in that one story such deep human realities as sex, violence and religion. It is indeed strange how these apparently opposite values can function together in the lives of some people. That is perhaps what the final redactor wanted us to discover and make us reflect upon, especially through repeating similar stories.

Not too many readers will take these chapters as history, and indeed the Samson story does not correspond at all to what one would expect of a history book. In these four chapters we find a great variety of literary genres, such as a marvellous annunciation story; stories of extraordinary exploits, such as Samson's fight with a lion and pushing a temple to ruins; stories about prostitutes; riddles; and more. Many such literary genres are popular, and people love to hear them. This may be the reason for the popularity of the Samson story among many readers even today. The story has also favourably been compared with several myths from other cultures. There is no doubt then that the Samson story is legendary, with perhaps a few historical elements about a popular hero of that time.

The story is obviously written from an Israelite perspective and intended for Israelite readers. Writer and readers may enjoy how Samson took revenge on the Philistines, which says something about them. But how would Philistine readers have reacted to this violent Samson? Clearly, a Philistine author could not have written about this man, in the eyes of some Israelites, perhaps, a hero, but in the eyes of the Philistines a bandit or what we might call a terrorist. The story of Samson, as we have it now, is written to entertain and to teach people in a subtle way. Some readers may be inclined to laugh with some of the adventures, enjoying this unique hero; they may look at it as a real comedy. But others may feel more like crying, seeing this story as a real tragedy. What a life completely spoiled, and what a death!

The Story of Samson

Before the Samson story proper we find an introductory statement: "Again the Israelites began to do what displeases the LORD, and the LORD delivered them into the hands of the Philistines for forty years" (13:1). This is the classical formula that introduces each of the major judges (3:7-8; 3:12; 4:1-2; etc.). It reaffirms the theme that summarizes that period of the history of Israel. After the Israelites settled in the Promised Land, their big temptation was idolatry, which is of course the greatest sin against the LORD, their God. That period is also characterized by continual problems with their neighbours, who do not want these newcomers to settle there. The biblical writer tries to understand the reason for these difficulties. According to his theology, he links them to Israel's idolatry. The LORD uses Israel's enemies to punish his unfaithful people. This time the oppressors are the Philistines who are known as "The Enemy" in Israel's history. They made the Israelites suffer; it took Israel years, even until the time of David, to master them. The oppression, says the text, lasted for "forty years." This is a well-known symbolic biblical number that corresponds to one generation. Israel, who became unfaithful to the LORD in the desert, had to stay there for forty years so that only the new generation could enter the Promised Land. The length of time of the oppression varies from judge to judge – for instance, eight years (3:8), eighteen years (3:14) or twenty years (4:3). But forty is much longer than in any of the other cases. The situation is a critical one. Israel is suffering from the oppression of its most dangerous enemy, and for a whole generation. As in all the preceding cases, Israel is in need of a judge, a deliverer, someone who can free the people from this inhuman oppression. In this terrible situation, that person must be extremely capable. An ordinary judge would not do.

In all other stories of oppression, Israel then cries to God for help and God answers by sending the deliverer (3:9, 15; etc.). This time is different. There is no cry of the people; the LORD intervenes directly and in a unique way.

Samson's story opens with an annunciation story. A divine messenger assures a barren woman that she will give birth to a son, whom she will call Samson. He is the only judge for whom we have a birth story (13:2-25), and his is one of the most beautiful biblical birth narratives. This seems to suggest then that in this hopeless situation there will finally be a real, true Judge, a Saviour, one who will end once and for all the suffering of his people. More is expected from him since he is the last of all the judges. It's now or never! Will this be the moment of total liberation, the reversal of all unfaithfulness and the time of complete salvation?

Manoah and his wife were a married couple living in Zorah. Like every other family at that time, they both must have been dreaming of having children, but she was barren. In other such cases, we find sadness, jealousy, humiliation. How these two people were coping with this painful test in their lives is not mentioned, nor is there any indication if they had tried human solutions, like Abraham and Sarah did (Genesis 16), or if they ever, like Anna, prayed to the LORD (1 Samuel 1:9). One day, out of nowhere, everything changes for them. A divine messenger appears to the woman with a great message: "You are barren and have had no child. But from now on take great care. Take no wine or strong drink, and eat nothing unclean. For you will conceive and bear a son. No razor is to touch his head, for the boy shall be God's nazirite from his mother's womb. It is he who will begin to rescue Israel from the power of the Philistines" (vv. 3-5). What a message! She who is barren will have a son, and Israel that is oppressed will gain some freedom through her son.

That son will be a nazirite, which means that he will be a man vowed and consecrated to the LORD. Another biblical text explains in detail what that implies: no touching, drinking or eating anything that comes from the vine; no razor may touch his hair, thus letting the hair grow; and finally not getting close to any corpse, since that will make him unclean. This commitment by a man or a woman was normally made for a particular period (Numbers 6:2-8). If the person did not observe one of these obligations, there was a ritual for the renewal of the consecration (Numbers 6:9-12). But for the son of Manoah and his wife it will be different, he will be a nazirite "from his mother's womb." For this reason, the mother has to observe these commitments during her pregnancy. This is obviously going to be a very special boy. He will not only be consecrated to the LORD, but he is also destined to play an important role for his people. His mission will be similar to that of all the other judges. He will bring freedom from oppression, but the messenger says, "he will begin to rescue Israel." The messenger does not directly say that her son will be a "judge," but he insists that he will be a "nazirite," a man consecrated to God. Could it be that the salvation this young man is supposed to bring to Israel will be of a different nature? Will he obtain it through a special intervention by God? Expectations increase even more.

The woman, who must be full of excitement, tells her husband what the divine messenger said, but adds an interesting detail. While the messenger had said that her son would be a nazirite "from his mother's womb," she adds "to his dying day" (v. 7). Although most people took that oath for a limited period, this boy will be consecrated to the LORD his whole life. It may be that the messenger really said that to the woman, or this may simply be her personal wish. When her husband hears this surprising news, he prays to God that the messenger will appear a second time to "instruct us in what we must do with the boy when he is born" (v. 8). They have never had children, so they have no experience in how to educate them, and they are probably getting on in years. Since this future son will be a nazirite from his mother's womb, they need some guidelines on their responsibilities towards the baby. Manoah's prayer is heard and the messenger appears a second time, but again to the woman alone. She invites her husband to join them, and he addresses his question directly to the messenger: "When your words are fulfilled, what is to be the boy's rule of life? How must we behave?" (v. 12). The messenger repeats the same basic message concerning the obligations that the boy will have to follow as a nazirite: "… let him obey all the orders I gave this woman" (v. 14).

There is certainly reason to celebrate and to thank the messenger. Manoah invites him to stay for a nice meal. The messenger refuses, suggesting that it would be better to prepare a sacrifice for the LORD, as it is the LORD who will cause this barren woman to bear a son.

And the promise comes true: "The woman gave birth to a son and called him Samson" (v. 24). Generally, in other marvellous birth narratives, the messenger of God determines the name that one of the parents must give their son (Genesis 16:11; 17:19; Isaiah 7:14). But here, the barren woman decides on the name "Samson," a diminutive of the Hebrew word for *sun*. Indeed, he is "Sunny Boy." What sunshine he promises to be in the life of these two people, and what a sunrise, a new day, seems to be in store for oppressed Israel!

This beautiful birth narrative ends with a few short promise statements (vv. 24-25). "The child grew" – what happens during the early years of the baby's life are unimportant; the writer wants to move quickly to what Samson will accomplish. "And the LORD blessed him." Samson, the fruit of a divine promise, is not left on his own after he is born; the LORD is with him. And "the spirit of the LORD began to move him…" The messenger had described Samson's mission, saying, "he will begin to rescue Israel from the power of the Philistines" (v. 5). The Philistines may have a lot of power, but Samson has the power of the spirit of the LORD upon him. That spirit "begins" to move Samson; everything seems in place for Samson to "begin" his work of salvation. Once more, the expectations continue to increase. We seem to have reached the moment of truth.

The reader is curious to find out what Samson's first activity will be and is looking forward to seeing how the hero will start his mission. This is described in the next episode (14:1-20). The story opens with "Samson went down to Timnah" (v. 1); it is a city that must have been under the control of the Philistines. To go down to one of the enemy cities seems to be a dangerous, but perhaps courageous thing for Samson to do. Is his first step to go right to one of their strongholds and so to confront the enemy? If that is what the reader expects, then he or she will soon be disappointed. Other things in life excite Samson more: "There he saw one of the daughters of the Philistines." There is nothing wrong with seeing a woman, but here it is more than just seeing her. The rest of the story shows that Samson wants her. There is nothing wrong with that, either, but the venom comes at the end of the sentence: this woman is a Philistine. Samson, whose mission is to begin saving Israel from the oppression of the Philistines, wants to take a woman of the enemy. A strange beginning! His mission does not seem to be his first priority.

Since, at that time, marriages had to be agreed upon between the parents of the two partners, Samson returns home and tells his father and mother, "At Timnah I saw one of the daughters of the Philistines. Take her for me, then, to be my wife" (v. 2). Samson wants the woman he has seen to be his wife. This all seems a little superficial. The text mentions twice that Samson has "seen" that woman, but mentions nothing else. Clearly, he is attracted by her appearance; indeed, a woman of another culture or tribe may seem exotic. The text does not even say if Samson has already spoken to her and if she is interested in him. It does not even tell us if he loves her. He wants her. He does not ask for any advice from his parents, nor does he search for their approval. He, the son, gives the orders to his parents: "take her for me." He needs to work through his parents since they have to do the deliberations with the parents of the girl concerning the possible dowry and other formalities of the marriage contract.

His parents are not keen to fulfill his request. They do not give a categorical "no" or "yes," but they respond with a question: "Is there no woman among those of your own clan or among your whole nation, for you to seek a wife among these uncircumcised Philistines?" (v. 3). These parents may sound very narrow minded and old-fashioned. Should they not be open to other cultures? But these parents have lived for a while, and they have observed that married life is not easy with a person of your own culture; how much more difficult it could be with a person of a totally different culture, especially one of the enemy clan. Samson asked for a woman of the Philistines, but the parents add something. In describing the Philistines as "uncircumcised," his parents are more or less saying the Philistines are pagans. How can a marriage work between a pious Israelite and a pagan woman? This is an even bigger problem for Samson, who is a nazirite. What Philistine woman could help her husband live up to his obligations of that consecration to the LORD? Samson's parents, having serious doubts about the wisdom of such a marriage, base themselves upon a centuries-old tradition. When Abraham was looking for the ideal wife for his son Isaac, he also wanted a woman from among his own clan and not from among the Canaanites, among whom he lived. He knew that marrying a Canaanite could cause for his son to fall into idolatry (Genesis 24:3-4). Many examples prove that danger. The best is Solomon, with his many foreign wives (1 Kings 11:1-13). It is not surprising that the Law of Moses forbade such marriages: "When the LORD your God has led you into the land… You must not marry with them: you must not give a daughter of yours to a son of theirs, not take a daughter of theirs for a son of yours, for this would turn away your son from following me to serving other gods…" (Deuteronomy 7:1-4). The parents have a serious and valid objection.

But Samson has made up his mind, and their objection does not affect him at all. He does not even seem to reflect upon their question. He immediately repeats his order: "Take this one for me; take her." That is the one he wants, and the reason he gives is "because I like her [literally, because she is pleasing in my eyes]" (v. 3). Samson shows how superficial he is: he wants her because she looks good. He saw her, he likes her and he asks to take her. He acts like the sons of God who " 'saw' that the daughters of men were pleasing, so they 'took' as many as they chose" (Genesis 6:2). This is also how David behaved: "he 'saw' from the roof a woman bathing… David sent messengers to 'take' her" (2 Samuel 11:2.4).

Samson does not use his head; he is overpowered by his passion. The son rejects the elementary rule of human wisdom: "Listen, my son, to your father's instruction, do not reject your mother's teaching" (Proverbs 1:8). He is not open to hearing their advice, and that is even worse when it concerns a foreign woman: "My son, if you take my words to heart… Keeping you from the alien woman, from the stranger… Of those who go to her not one returns…" (Proverbs 2:1, 16, 19). Samson does not listen, even though marrying a foreigner goes directly against the divine law.

This law applies to any person in Israel, and especially to a nazirite, consecrated to God from his mother's womb until his death!

But Samson has the last word. Should his parents have been more directive and refused his request? But they have only one son. Perhaps they were afraid to refuse him categorically, since that could lead to a permanent break in the relationship, as sometimes happens in families. Or maybe they wanted to be respectful towards him and, after outlining the dangers of this decision, left it to him. After all, it is his life. We as readers can interpret his parents' reaction in many ways. But whatever their reason, they gave in to his demands. Time would tell if they did the right thing.

Samson, having made his decision, "went down to Timnah." Once again he risks himself in the territory of the Philistines. Before arriving in the town "he reached the vineyards of Timnah." Why would a nazirite, who is not supposed to touch anything that is connected with the vine, go into a vineyard? Samson apparently loves to play with danger and temptation. And indeed he is in danger: "he saw a young lion coming roaring towards him" (v. 5). A lion in other biblical stories can be a symbol for God's anger against his unfaithful people (Amos 1:2; 5:19). A good example is the lion that devoured the disobedient prophet (1 Kings 13). This appearance of the lion in the vineyards of Timnah may well be a clear warning from the LORD to stop Samson in his project, which is contrary to the law of God and to the advice of his parents. But that is not how Samson reads it; in fact, he moves straight towards the lion. For the first time he shows his extraordinary strength: with "no weapon in his hand he tore the lion in pieces." He could do that, says the narrator, because "the spirit of the LORD seized on him." In the stories of the other judges, that expression is often used to explain how a particular judge could free Israel from its oppressors (3:10; 6:34; 11:29). Here, however, Samson's power has nothing to do with his mission for the salvation of his people; he uses it for his own safety. The narrator adds that Samson did not tell his parents what he had done (v. 6), for good reason. They would have understood God's warning, and it would have confirmed them in their conviction that a Philistine woman was not for Samson.

Divine warning or not, not even a lion can stop Samson, and he continues on his road: "he went down and talked to the woman, and he liked her [literally, she was pleasing in his eyes]" (v. 7). The first time Samson had only "seen" the woman, and "she was pleasing in his eyes" (v. 3); now he "speaks" to her, and that confirms his appreciation of her.

Samson is determined to pursue this woman. "A few days later he came back to take her" (v. 8). Twice he had asked his parents to "take" her but he no longer waits for them to do so; he does it himself. But when he returns to the woman to marry her, he makes another detour: "he went out of his way to look at the carcass of the lion, and there was a swarm of bees in the lion's body, and honey" (v. 8). He first sees the bees; they are of course not as dangerous as a lion, but they can cause much harm if one comes too close. Bees are rarely mentioned in the Bible, but they can represent the enemies that the LORD sends against his people (Isaiah 7:18). The lion had been the LORD's first warning to stop Samson from marrying the Philistine woman; the second is not to touch the carcass. A nazirite had no right to go near a corpse, since that would make him unclean (Numbers 6:6). But after he has seen the bees, Samson notices that there is honey in the dead lion's body. Just as the lion did not stop him, the bees do not stop him: "he took up some honey in his hand and ate it as he went along" (v. 9). Samson not only transgresses his obligations as a nazirite by approaching and touching a dead animal, he eats something taken from the carcass, which was forbidden to all Israelites (Leviticus 11:24-28, 31-40). Samson cannot resist the tempting delicacy of honey, just like he could not resist the beautiful woman.

It gets worse. Samson does not limit himself to his personal transgression; "he gave some to his parents, which they ate too." It is the story of paradise and the forbidden fruit all over again: "the woman took some of its fruit and ate it. She gave some to her husband who was with her, and he ate it" (Genesis 3:6). But there is a big difference between the two stories. Adam knew about the fruit, but Samson's parents did not know where the honey came from: "he did not tell them he had taken it from the lion's carcass" (v. 9), just as he did not tell them about his killing of the lion (v. 6). This pious father and mother are unaware that they are eating something unclean, forbidden by the law, offered to them by their nazirite son. Samson here treats his parents, and especially his mother, very unfairly, since during her pregnancy she had observed all the requirements of a nazirite (13:4). Even though Samson rejected his parents' advice, he could at least have respected their religious convictions. It looks as if he is making a joke of their piety. He misleads them, and for what reason? Nothing seems to justify this behaviour.

In any case, now the wedding is on and the party can start (14:10-20). "Then he went down to the woman, and they made a feast for Samson for seven days there, for such is the custom of young men" (v. 10). Of course there is nothing wrong with celebrating a marriage. But the English translation does not reveal the seriousness of what is happening. It simply says a "feast," but the Hebrew word is the word to describe a party where plenty of wine is consumed. Samson has gone against his parents' advice and against the divine law by marrying this Philistine woman. He also has not respected on of his oaths as a nazirite, making himself unclean by approaching the carcass of the lion and by eating the honey from it. Now he goes against another of his commitments, for he was supposed to abstain from wine. It is not even a case of taking a small glass; the drinking party goes on for seven days, according to the custom of the Philistines! Samson is obviously more concerned about following the customs of these uncircumcised people than respecting his obligations as a nazirite.

Samson had said nothing to his parents about his exploit of killing the lion, but he had talked to the woman (vv. 6-7) and we can easily guess that he told her that story to impress her. Such 'heroic' action must not have gone unnoticed; consequently, these Philistines are on their guard against this strange Israelite who is marrying one of their girls. And so, "because they were frightened of him, they chose thirty companions to stay with him" (v. 11). They want to be sure that nothing will happen during this wedding feast. They even may wonder if this marriage was not just a trick of Samson's to enter into their ranks; after all, they are enemies.

Samson, in the middle of enemy territory, is not impressed at being surrounded by guards. At parties, people often love to play games. Samson proposes one to his thirty bodyguards: "Let me ask you a riddle. If you find the answer within the seven days of the feast, I will give thirty pieces of fine linen and thirty robes. But if you cannot find the answer, then you in your turn must give me thirty pieces of fine linen and thirty festal robes" (vv. 12-13). That seems a fair deal. At least one of these thirty Philistines should be capable of finding the answer, and even if they cannot, then the most each one has to give is one piece of fine linen and a robe to Samson. Of course, if Samson loses, he will have to pay a fair amount of money to fulfill his part. It may appear tempting to accept, but should they not have been a little suspicious that Samson is ready to take such a costly risk? And there comes the riddle: "Out of the eater came what is eaten, and out of the strong came what is sweet" (v. 14). Not bad for Samson to have invented a riddle that nearly seems unsolvable. He is not only strong; he is also rather clever. For the reader it is easy enough to answer the riddle after hearing the story of the lion with the honey inside, but who else would think of that?

Three days of the feast pass, and nobody knows the answer to the riddle. Samson must have been in his glory while drinking more wine. The men become nervous; time is going fast, and only four days are left to find the answer. So they use a trick. On the fourth day they go to Samson's wife and say: "Seduce your husband into telling you the answer to the riddle, or we will burn you and your father's house together. Did you invite us here to rob us?" (v. 15).

They certainly mean business. The woman is faced with a difficult decision: for her and even for her parents it is a matter of life and death. And so she accepts and approaches Samson in tears: "You only hate me, you do not love me. You have asked my fellow countrymen a riddle and not even told me the answer" (v. 16). For the first time in the relationship between Samson and his wife, love is mentioned. Can we speak of love in that marriage? Samson offers a reasonable answer. Since he did not reveal the answer even to his parents, why is she surprised that he did not tell it to her either? But the woman does not give up. After all, her life and the life of her father are at stake, while for her husband, whom she hardly knows, it is only a question of money. And so the strong Samson – who can defeat a lion, but who cannot resist the sweetness of honey – gives into her tears. On the seventh day he gives her the answer, and she tells it to her "countrymen" (v. 17). She clearly shows where her attachments lie, and there goes the "love" for her husband that she had been asking for.

Samson is a sore loser. Understandably, he got angry. He could have been angry at his wife for having cheated him, or at the men for having used his wife, or at himself for having given in to his wife. But instead he does something shocking. "The spirit of the LORD seized on him" – as we have seen, that "spirit" has nothing spiritual about it; it refers to special physical strength. And "he went down to Ashkelon, killed thirty men there, took what they wore and gave the festal robes to those who had answered the riddle" (v. 19). He kills thirty innocent people of another Philistine town who had nothing to do with the story! Samson, whose mission is supposed to be "to begin to rescue Israel from the power of the Philistines" (13:5), uses his extraordinary strength to kill people only so he can pay his debt. And once again this nazirite becomes unclean by touching the corpses to deprive them of their robes. Some hero! How will that help his mission? It can only increase the oppression that the Philistines continue to impose upon Israel.

The end of the wedding feast is even more bizarre. After this "heroic" exploit, Samson "burning with rage returned to his father's house" (v. 19). This is certainly the best thing to do. In Timnah, a town under control of the Philistines, he is no longer safe. And because he left, it is understandable that "Samson's wife was given to the companion who had been his best man" (v. 20). Rather humiliating for Samson, but luckily, that is something he does not know. For the woman it is very fortunate; she has a new husband. And that is the end of Samson's marriage! It turns out that the divine law against marriage with foreigners and his parent's advice not to marry a daughter of the Philistines were not that bad after all. Samson has learned that lesson the hard way. Or has he? For the story is not over yet.

One day Samson "went back to see his wife." That visit ends up in another disaster (15:1-8). The lesson he learned earlier was clearly not enough for Samson. He must have kept dreaming about this woman who had been so pleasing in his eyes, even after she betrayed him by seducing him to make him reveal the answer to his riddle. He must have wondered how she would react to his visit, and so this violent Samson appears to have become a gentleman: "he had brought a kid for her." A little gift can heal some wounds. He may have come to excuse himself for his rude behaviour, to admit he had not accepted that he lost in the riddle contest, that he had acted in such a barbarian way by killing some of her compatriots, or that he had broken up the marriage feast. But these are not the reasons for his visit. On arrival, he divulges his real intention: "I wish to go to my wife in her bedroom." He wants sex. His parents had been the first to oppose his marriage, but now her father objects. He does not let Samson enter the room, saying, "I felt sure that you had taken a real dislike to her, so I gave her to your companion" (v. 2). What the reader already knows is now revealed to Samson. This news comes as a shock, and a very humiliating one at that. The father-in-law, knowing Samson's violent character, tries to calm him down, saying, "But would not her younger sister suit you better? Have her instead of the other." Just as his parents, in trying to dissuade him from marrying a Philistine, had made him a counterproposal to take a wife from his own people, here also the father-in-law makes a counterproposal that he considers very fair. He offers his younger daughter; she could be more appealing.

But when Samson has set his mind on something, no one is going to talk him out of it. He wants that woman. He refused his parents' advice earlier, and now he refuses his father-in-law's offer. Since he cannot have his wife back, he turns to the only other solution he Samson knows: violence. "I can only get my own back on the Philistines now by doing them some damage" (v. 3). We expect him to go after his best man, who now is the new husband of his former wife. That would have been at least a little understandable; the world is regrettably full of such dramatic triangle stories, when the ex kills the new lover of the woman. Or Samson could have taken revenge against his father-in-law, who had given his wife to another man. But instead, once again Samson goes after the innocent. In no time Samson catches 300 foxes, turns them tail to tail, puts burning torches between each pair of tails, and sets them loose in the fields of the Philistines. What a strange and dangerous imagination he has! And since he had come to see his wife at harvest time (v. 1), the damage is tremendous. "In this way he burned both sheaves and standing corn, and the vines and olive trees as well" (v. 5). All those farmers who worked hard to have a good harvest see it all go up in flames; their vines and olive trees that take generations to grow and to become productive are destroyed in a few moments. The future of all these people is famine and misery. How does that help Samson get what he wants, which is to get his wife back? His revenge is out of proportion.

Violence creates more violence. When these Philistine farmers try to discover who could be behind such a crime, they receive the answer "Samson, who married the Timnite's daughter, his father-in-law took the wife back again and gave her to his companion instead" (v. 6). But the informants leave out several important elements of the story. First, Samson had left his wife, and the father-in-law, concluding that Samson was gone for good, had in good conscience given his daughter to another man. In addition, although the father-in-law had offered his younger daughter to Samson in his other daughter's place, Samson had refused the offer. A half-truth is always dangerous. The father-in-law is not to blame, nor is the woman, who may not even have known everything that went on. The guilty party is Samson, and the farmers know that. He is the one who burned the fields. We would expect them to go after him. But just as Samson took revenge on innocent people, the farmers do the same: "the Philistines burned the woman and her family to death" (v. 6). Were they afraid to touch Samson?

Amidst this violence against innocent people, has "justice" been restored? Samson took revenge and then the Philistines took revenge, so they are even. But this is not how it works. Violence begets violence. It becomes a cycle that is hard to stop. And now the ball is back in Samson's court, and this is what he decides: "Since this is how you behave, I swear I will not rest till I have had my revenge on you" (v. 7). He is upset – probably not about the death of his father-in-law, whom he must have considered an obstacle to getting his wife back – but about the death of the woman who was so pleasing in his eyes. All hope to recover her is gone for good. Samson does not wait long to act upon his decision: "He fell on them for all he was worth and caused great havoc" (v. 8). Once again he wants the last word, in the form of brutal and far-reaching violence. The Philistines, in their revenge, had been more restrained. Samson leaves Timnah now: this time, he does not return to his father's house, but "he went down to the cave in the Rock of Etam," a place in Judah's territory, and "he stayed there." He knows that the Philistines are not going to rest and accept their last humiliation, so he seeks the protection of a cave. He hides; he is no longer living in the light, but in the darkness. The dead are buried in caves; he is like a living dead person.

But Samson is not dead yet, as the following story shows. Whereas the preceding stories happened in Timnah, a city under Philistine control (14:1–15:8), the action of the next story moves to Judah (15:9-20). The Philistines came up and encamped in Judah in a place called Lehi. After Samson had burned all their fields, they had to go somewhere to survive and to find food. But the men of Judah, which is still under the domination of the Philistines (13:1), realize that the arrival of such a group of Philistines spells trouble. They ask them, full of fear: "Why are you attacking us?" After all, they have done nothing wrong. The answer is short and clear: "We have come to bind Samson and to do to him what he did to us" (v. 10). The intention of the Philistines is not to cause further damage to the people of Judah; they only want Samson. Their statement contains the principle that is behind the actions of the two protagonists and that dominates the whole story. When Samson did not get his wife back, he could only think of "doing them (Philistines) some damage" (v. 3). He, therefore, had burnt their fields. In response, the Philistines asked, "Who has done this?" (v. 6).

Then they took revenge by burning Samson's wife and her father. Upon which Samson had said, "Since this is what you have done" (v. 7) and took his next revenge. It is now the turn of the Philistines, and indeed that is how they see it: we will "do to him what he did to us." Will there ever be an end to the spiral of violence? But unlike Samson, who often took revenge on innocent people, the Philistines this time are after the guilty one.

The people of Judah have suffered enough from the Philistine oppression. None of Samson's actions have given them any relief; on the contrary, these personal revenges of his may ultimately increase their suffering. That does not make any sense. Why would the people have to pay for Samson's stupidities? The people decide not to take this any longer. They go down to the cave where Samson is hiding and challenge him: "Do you not know that the Philistines have us in their power? Now what have you done to us?" (v. 11). What Samson did to the Philistines ends up being done to his own people. Here is the tragedy or the irony of the Samson story. His mission is "to begin to rescue Israel from the power of the Philistines" (v. 5); not only has he not even begun to do so, he has increased the oppression. His answer to his own people is empty. He does not admit to the consequences of his actions, but selfishly states, "What they did to me I did to them" (v. 11). Even these words are untrue: he always did more to them than what they did to him. His revenge was always without restrictions.

The people are not at all convinced by Samson's answer, and decide that he must bear the consequences of his actions so the whole people does not have to pay for them. "We have come down to bind you, to hand you over to the Philistines" (v. 12). And they mean business: they are three thousand men strong! To the surprise of the reader and the men of Judah, Samson becomes like a lamb. The one who had never accepted the advice of anybody, neither of his parents nor of his father-in-law, accepts their proposal without resistance. This is probably the only reasonable thing Samson has ever done. But he asks for one favour: "Swear to me not to kill me yourselves." That indeed would have been too great a humiliation for this violent man. The people accept this condition easily, since it was never their intention to kill him. All they want is to free themselves from him and to hand him over to the Philistines. And so "they bound him with two new ropes and brought him up from the Rock" (v. 13).

This person who was called to liberate Israel from the oppression of the Philistines, who is now bound by his own people and handed over to the Philistines. What a strange twist in the Samson story. The Philistines have reason to rejoice, and when they see the terrorist bound by his own people being brought to them, "they came running towards him with triumphant shouts" (v. 14). Finally, they are the victors. But a person who can kill a lion with his hands, can easily break a few ropes, even new ones. Samson recovers his magic powers – "the spirit of the Lord seized on Samson" – and the ropes melted off his hands (v. 14). Samson is a free man again. But, being who he is, how could he leave it at that? "Catching sight of the fresh jawbone of a donkey, he reached out and snatched it up." Once again, the nazirite does not hesitate to touch a dead animal. He does not care if that makes him unclean. All he knows is that with that donkey's jawbone he can kill, and so "with it he struck down a thousand men" (v. 15). He even composes a poem to sing his own 'heroic' deed (v. 16). In that he resembles Lamech, who also composed a poem to sing his pride at having taken revenge without any limitations (Genesis 4:23-24).

After such emotions and exploits it is not surprising that Samson got "thirsty." And now, for the first time in his life, Samson does something that nobody would expect of him: "he called on the Lord." Samson prays (v. 18). This story has it all – sex, violence and now God. Samson can control many things, he can master people and a lion, but he cannot control nature. Only God is the master of nature, and Samson seems to know that. He suddenly needs God to survive. The prayer is short. Samson starts by trying to please God by giving him all the honours: "You yourself have worked this great victory by the hand of your servant." He now ascribes to God his 'heroic' deed. He even dares to call himself God's servant, a title that is reserved for the great men of the Bible. After all, he is a person consecrated to God, he is a nazirite. That may come handy as a good bargaining tool. After singing God's praises, Samson moves to his request, which is manipulative: "and now must I die of thirst and fall into the hands of the uncircumcised?" Samson begs to live. He does not want to die of thirst or become so weak that the Philistines could kill him. Until now, he has always spoken of the "Philistines," but now he describes them as the "uncircumcised," which is what his father called them. He, the nazirite, is the "servant of the LORD," the good guy; they are the "uncircumcised," the pagans, the bad guys.

And the LORD listens to Samson's first prayer, because he is a God of the living. God does not want Samson to die of thirst or to be killed by the Philistines. He is a God who welcomes the person for who he is, with all his imperfections, and who hears the human prayer, even the rather selfish kind. "God opened a hollow in the ground… and water gushed out of it. Samson drank." And after Samson drinks, two things happen to him: "his spirit returned and he revived" (v. 19). The one who was close to death comes back to life. Earlier in the story, "the spirit of the LORD" had come upon Samson (v. 14); now "his spirit returned." But that is not very promising. It seems that Samson returns to his own self, how he normally is, not like he was in this sole moment of piety.

And indeed, the rest of the story will prove that Samson has remained the same; nothing has changed deep down in him. What follows (ch. 16) is a repeat of what we read in the preceding stories (ch. 14–15). It is like a second edition, corrected and augmented.

Samson's piety does not last. He has been without a woman for a long time, and wants sex (16:1-3). Immediately after God has heard his prayer and saved him from dying of thirst, the first thing Samson does is not pray a prayer of thanksgiving. Instead, "from here Samson went to Gaza, and seeing a harlot there he went into her house" (v. 1). Samson is incorrigible! He did not learn anything of his experience in Timnah. In Gaza, one of the five major cities of the Philistines, he seems to go looking for trouble and danger. Although he claims to despise them, referring to them as uncircumcised in a prayer to God, he does not despise their women. In fact, they seem to have a special attraction for him. The first time he sees a woman, she is pleasing to his eyes, but this time, he is not concerned with finding one who is pleasing; he simply goes to a harlot.

Harlots are public figures; the men of Gaza know that "Samson has arrived." He had succeeded in escaping from the Philistines last time, now he is caught; he is in one of their key towns. They surround the place and keep watch over him the whole night, thinking, "we will wait till daybreak; then we will kill him" (v. 2). Let him have his sex, even all night long if he wants. He will be so exhausted that he will be easy prey, as he will no longer have his extraordinary strength. They are certain that they have their chance to finish him off. Samson, however, may be a violent person, a womanizer, and may at times act like a fool, but he is not completely stupid. Whether he was informed that he was in danger or by chance, he escapes: "Samson however stayed in bed till midnight." After having had a few hours of pleasure, he is satisfied and gets up. But how could he leave Gaza without doing some violence? He cannot resist. The text does not speak of the spirit of the LORD, as on other occasions (14:6, 19; 15:14); Samson simply, under his own strength, dismantles the whole city gate and carries it to Hebron (v. 3). Why he brings it there is not said, but the people of Judah who had handed him over to the Philistines must have been surprised to see him arriving with the city gate of Gaza! At least this time Samson did not make any human victims, but what a humiliation for the Philistines. How happy Samson must be of his 'heroic' action. He has freed himself from their hands, but how does this action free Israel from the oppression of the Philistines? In fact, the people of Hebron have reason to fear a counterattack by the Philistines from Gaza.

But in the next story Samson will be the loser; it will be his Waterloo (16:4–22). It starts once again with the sex theme: "After this, Samson fell in love with a woman in the Vale of Sorek" (v. 4). In his previous liaisons with women, the text tells us he had "seen" them. This time it is different; he loves this woman. Samson has perhaps matured; his attraction to women is less superficial and he is in love. This encounter happens in the "Vale of Sorek," which means the valley of choice vines, which is perhaps a little suspect for a nazirite who had to abstain from everything connected with vines. Unlike the two previous women, who remained nameless, this woman has a name: "Delilah." The meaning of the name is not totally clear, but it resembles the Hebrew word for night. So there is Sunny Boy in love with Lady of the Night! Even if it is not said explicitly, could the name suggest that she also is a harlot? She certainly does not despise money, as the rest of the story shows.

Once more it does not take long for the people to know that Samson the terrorist is around. Instead of surrounding the place with guards like the people of Gaza did, the Philistines try another tactic. "The chiefs of the Philistines visited her [Delilah] and said to her, 'Seduce him and find out where his great strength comes from, and how we can master him and bind him and reduce him to helplessness. In return we will each give you eleven hundred silver shekels'" (v. 5). They ask her for the same service that the bodyguards in Timnah had asked of Samson's wife: "Seduce him" (14:15). Seducing Samson does not seem to be too difficult. He is a strong man but very weak in the hands of a woman. The first time, in Timnah, he had not resisted, so we expect him to give in this time, too. The Philistines want their man alive: the reward offered to the woman is out of this world. Each of the chiefs of the five major cities of the Philistines offers 1100 silver shekels, for a total of 5500 shekels. That will motivate her to succeed. Samson may well love Delilah, but she seems to prefer her own people and, above all, the big money.

And so Delilah tries her chance (vv. 6-9). She says to Samson: "Please tell me where your great strength comes from, and what would be needed to bind you and tame you." Does Samson not suspect something? Did he not learn from his bad experience with his wife, who through seduction tried to discover his secret in the riddle contest? Samson enters the game and answers: "If I were bound with seven new bowstrings that had not yet been dried; I should lose my strength and become like any other man." This answer seems acceptable. Indeed, seven new, not dried, strings should do the job. Delilah must have given the answer to the chiefs of the Philistines, for they bring her the strings and she binds Samson with them. She also conceals some men in her room and then shouts to Samson, "The Philistines are on you, Samson!" But what are a few strings for Samson? He knew it would take more than that. He had proven it when the men of Judah had bound him with two new ropes to deliver him in the hands of the Philistines (15:14). In no time he is again a free man and "so the secret of his strength remained unknown." Funny game!

But Delilah does not give up; after all, there is a lot of money involved. It is worth another try (vv. 10-12). By now it is evident that she in not at all in love with him; she would rather have the money. But she knows that Samson is in love with her, so she tries to play on that and makes him feel guilty: "You have been laughing at me and telling me lies. But please tell me what would be needed to bind you." Delilah must not have left it at words; after all, she had been asked to seduce him, and so a few of her favours must have been more effective. And since we are in the valley of the choice vines, who knows? A little glass of wine might also help loose the nazirite's tongue so he reveals his secret. Samson must be completely stupid if he does not see what is happening, but he continues the game. He even seems to enjoy it. He now suggests that new ropes would be needed to bind him. The same story is repeated. When the men hiding in Delilah's room come out, Samson frees himself easily. He must enjoy how he dominates the situation.

The offered reward is high and very tempting, so Delilah makes a third attempt (vv. 13-14). The third time may be the lucky one! She accuses Samson again: "Up to now you have been laughing at me and telling me lies. Tell me what would be needed to bind you." This time Samson proposes something totally different: no strings, no ropes. "If you wove the seven locks of my hair into the wrap of the web and fixed the peg firmly, then I should lose my strength." That sounds new, and Delilah seems to believe it. "She lulled him to sleep, then wove the seven locks of his hair into the warp." Samson enjoys this, falling asleep in her lap and letting her play with his hair. That feels good! But he has become too daring. The mystery surrounding his strength is indeed in his hair. Again the Philistines come out, but Samson pulled out stuff and peg. "So the secret of his strength remained unknown."

Delilah realizes she has come closer to finding out true answer. She therefore tries a fourth time to discover his secret. Three is a perfect number; four is three plus one, so surely it would work this time (vv. 15-20). She changes her strategy and especially her accusation: "How can you say you love me when you do not trust me? Three times now you have laughed at me and have not told me where your great strength comes from." Samson must have told her he was in love with her and shown it to her in several ways; now, she plays on his love. Samson is deeply touched; he wants to prove to her that he really loves her. Samson's wife, too, had played on his feelings for her to obtain, at the last minute, the answer to the riddle. She had said, "You only hate me, you do not love me" (14:16). Then she had also persisted with her demand for several days, and had cried tears on his neck. Delilah does the same. "And day after day she persisted with her questions, and allowed him no rest, till he grew tired to death of it." The game is becoming less amusing.

Samson does not want to lose Delilah, even if that means disregarding the only oath as a nazirite that he has kept faithfully until now. So he tells her: "A razor has never touched my head, because I have been God's nazirite from my mother's womb. If my head were shorn, then my power would leave me and I should lose my strength and become like any other man" (v. 15; see 13:5). Samson, for the first time in his life, confesses that he is a nazirite, a person consecrated to God. He has taken a lot of freedom with the obligations of his oath. He has touched corpses and become unclean; he has also been drunk and touched products of the vine. But who would know that? He had made sure not to tell such things to his parents. Cutting his hair, of course, would have been noticed right away. Perhaps he wanted to appear committed to his vow to please his pious parents. But now he is ready to let go even of that. He wants Delilah. She is more important to him than an oath to the LORD, more important than what people, his parents included, may think of him.

This time, "Delilah realized he had told his whole secret to her" and she calls the chiefs: "Come just once more: he told his whole secret to me." The chiefs of the Philistines do not have to be pressed to come; there they are "with the money in their hands." Money has once more destroyed a human relationship, but that does not bother these Philistines. They trust that they finally have what they want; they will have Samson alive. So, like the time before, Delilah "lulled Samson to sleep in her lap." It still feels so good to Samson to be close to the woman he loves. "She summoned a man, and she sheared the seven locks off his head." Samson again enjoys feeling her hands in his hair. But while he is enjoying her touch, something dramatic is happening to him: "Then he began to lose his strength, and his power left him." When she cries out that the Philistines are on him, Samson is convinced that he will free himself easily, as he did before, and that the teasing love game can continue. But "he did not know that the LORD had turned away from him" (v. 20). Suddenly a new actor appears in the story: the LORD. He had been there all along, but no one had ever mentioned him or had taken notice of him. Samson had prayed to him once, but he had transgressed God's law. He had not observed two of his commitments as a nazarite, and now he has disregarded the last one. The LORD has shown patience with Samson for so long, but that is over, just as the whole love story with Delilah is over. She disappears completely from the scene; after all, she has her money. What does she care about Samson? Compare the beginning of Samson's adult life and its end. In the beginning, the LORD had "blessed him" and the spirit of the LORD "began" to move him (13:24–25). Now, at the end of the story, Samson "began" to lose his strength, and the LORD had "turned away" from him. In Delilah's lap, Samson has lost the LORD's blessing.

The game is over: "The Philistines seized him, put out his eyes and took him down to Gaza. They fettered him with a double chain of bronze, and he spent his time turning the mill in the prison" (v. 21). The Philistines are the big winners. Samson is the loser. He has lost the LORD; he has lost Delilah; he has even lost his eyes, which he used to "see" women. He will never see these attractive Philistine women again. He has lost his strength bound in a double chain of bronze. He has lost his freedom by being kept in a prison. He has even lost all human dignity by doing the work of an animal. The Philistines did not kill Samson. They have him alive, as they wanted; they can humiliate and torture him. To make the situation even more tragic, he is kept in Gaza, the city whose main gate he had dismantled and moved to Hebron. This last verse summarizes the irony of the whole Samson story. He was supposed to be a judge with a mission to begin to rescue Israel from the power of the Philistines, but ends up their prisoner. He is the only judge ever to have fallen into the hands of the enemy.

The story, however, ends with a little note: "But the hair that had been shorn off began to grow again" (v. 22). Note that after his hair had been shaved, he "began" to lose his strength (v. 19); now his hair "began" to grow. Apparently, the last word about Samson has not been said yet! Indeed, the story goes on to describe the strange death of this man whose life had also been rather strange (16:23-31). The chiefs of the Philistines, who had succeeded through Delilah in capturing him alive, now have reason to rejoice. They offer a great sacrifice to their god. They sing to their god, "Into our hands our god has delivered Samson our enemy" (v. 23). The whole people of the Philistines joins in the song. Everyone is full of joy, and they decide to amuse themselves even more at the expense of Samson, whom they now have under control safe in their prison: "Send Samson out to amuse us." Could it be more exciting? This blinded terrorist now performs "feats for them." The place is packed: "the building was crowded with men and women. All the chiefs of the Philistines were there, while about three thousand men and women were watching Samson's feats from the roof" (v. 27). What a delightful spectacle! One can only imagine Samson's humiliation, he who had loved humiliating the Philistines. Of course, the only thing that goes through his head is what has dominated his whole life: revenge. This blind strong man who is now playing the clown asks a boy who is leading him by the hand to bring him to the pillars supporting the building so he can lean against them.

And then Samson does something he has done only once before in his life: he prays. The first time he prayed because he was afraid he would die of thirst and did not want to fall into the hands of the Philistines (15:18). Now he is in their hands, and life has no meaning anymore for this proud man who always wanted to have the last word. Death seems preferable to life, but only on condition that he still could take revenge. He does not reveal in his prayer how he is planning to take this revenge, but prays, "Lord, I beg you, remember me; give me strength again this once, and let me be revenged on the Philistines at one blow for my two eyes" (v. 28). What satisfaction that would give him at the end of his life! After the first prayer the text says explicitly that God heard his prayer. This time it is left wide open. Did God hear him or did he leave Samson to himself? The text does not say either that the spirit of the LORD came upon Samson, like it had before, to give him strength. So there is Samson, all alone, holding the pillars like he had once grasped the gate of Gaza. He utters a wild cry: "May I die with the Philistines!" To him, death is preferable to life, especially if it allows him to take revenge and have the last word. He is not used to being under others' control. As he pushes and pushes with his brute, blind strength, the building collapses.

What did Samson accomplish? "Those he killed at his death outnumbered those he had killed in his life" (v. 30) and he had killed many in his lifetime (14:19; 15:8, 15). That joyful celebration of the Philistines in Gaza ends in tragedy. But this last 'heroic' action of Samson does not cause joy in the camp of Israel either. There are no celebrations; there is only a funeral without any honours. It is all done in the most discreet way, as if to forget the tragedy as soon as possible. There are no winners; all sides are losers. "His brothers and his father's whole family came down and carried him away. They took him up and buried him between Zorah and Eshtaol in the tomb of Manoah his father" (v. 31). The story thus returns to where it all had started, Samson is buried where he was born (13:2, 25), and what did he accomplish in between?

Theological Conclusion

What a tragedy the story of Samson is, and what a failed judge he is! The mission of all judges was to liberate Israel from oppression. Samson's mission was even more discrete: for him it was only "to begin to rescue Israel from the power of the Philistines" (13:5) who were dominating Israel for forty years (13:1). It is said twice that he was judge for twenty years (15:20; 16:31); he was thus active for a rather long period. And what did he accomplish in these twenty years? He did not even begin to rescue his people.

The difference between Samson and the other judges speaks for itself. This becomes very clear if one compares him, for example, with Othniel, the first major judge (Judges 3:7-11). Israel was then under the domination of Aram for eight years: look at what this Othniel accomplished as judge. "The spirit of the LORD came on him; he became judge in Israel and set out to fight. the LORD delivered the king of Aram, Cushan-rishathaim, into his hands, and he overcame Cushan-rishathaim. Then the land enjoyed rest for forty years." This success story speaks volumes compared to the failure story of Samson.

With or without the spirit of the LORD, Samson never fights the Philistines to free his people but always and only to take revenge for his own personal interests. The Aramaeans fell into the hands of Othniel; some of the Philistines also fell a few times into the hands of Samson, but he ended up in their hands, in their prison. He is the only judge to whom this happened. Even worse, he even fell into the hands of the men of Judah, his own people – which is unthinkable for any judge – and his own people handed him over to the Philistines. He did not appear to his people as their deliverer; on the contrary, his 'heroic' actions put his people in danger of being even more oppressed by the Philistines. After the interventions of the other judges, the land enjoyed rest for a number of years (Judges 3:11, 30; 5:31; 8:28). Nothing like this happened after Samson's adventures. In fact, he was a judge for twenty years, while the oppression of the Philistines lasted double that number of years. It must have continued after Samson's death; most likely the Philistines increased even more severely their domination over Israel because of Samson's wild and unlimited revenge on them.

This biblical Tarzan was a total failure as a judge. Predestined by God to be a nazirite from his mother's womb until his death, and to become a deliverer of his people, he neglected the obligations of his consecration. What is more, Samson does not seem to learn from his bad experiences, as the text illustrates marvellously. Sex and violence dominate his life. He knows only one principle: "What they did to me, I did to them" (15:11). And yet he does much worse than what is done to him, and takes revenge on innocent people.

God is not the centre of Samson's life. Only twice does the text tell us he prays to God, and his prayers are selfish ones. Samson has offended God, caused his parents to suffer, used several women to satisfy his own passion and, put his own people in danger, and killed thousands of Philistines without providing any lasting peace. What a spoiled life, and what a useless death. Samson is not a hero but a fool. His story is a forceful and tragic reminder of where squandered potential can lead. What a failed judge of Israel! Not surprisingly, he is the last of the judges, unlucky number thirteen. Israel needed a change.

3

SAUL: A Failed King
(1 Samuel 9 – 2 Samuel 1)

Critical Observations

S aul is mentioned for the first time in 1 Samuel 9, where he is chosen to become the first king of Israel. His death is reported in 1 Samuel 31. This, then, gives the beginning and the end of Saul's story. But 2 Samuel 1, which describes how David hears about Saul's death and then gives his elegy over Saul and Jonathan, could also be considered part of that story. A major section of the Bible is thus dedicated to this intriguing person, Saul.

The texts of the Saul story, like so often happens in the Bible, raise all kind of issues for the critical reader. The same event, or at least similar events, is reported more than once. Saul is anointed by Samuel to be the leader of Israel (9:3–10:16); but in another section Saul is chosen king by lot (10:17-27), and in still another, the people proclaim Saul as their king after his victory over the Ammonites (11:1-15). Samuel breaks twice with Saul (13:8-15; 15:10-23). David enters Saul's court as a harp player (16:14-23), but in the following chapter, when Saul sees David fighting Goliath, he wonders who this young boy is. David now enters Saul's court because of his military exploits (17:1-39). Saul tries twice to kill David with his spear, but David escapes each time (18:10-11; 19:9-10). David, meanwhile, could have killed Saul twice, but both times he spares the king (ch. 24 and 26). One text presents the death of Saul as a suicide (ch. 31), while in another text the soldier who reports Saul's death to David, admits to killing Saul (2 Samuel 1:1-16). Such doublets, tensions and contradictions are common in many biblical stories, and are proof of the complex origin of the story. They are generally explained as coming from different sources, traditions, layers or editions. Such explanations belong to diachronic approaches to the Scriptures; synchronic approaches, on the other hand, often demonstrate that there is more harmony between even conflicting texts than we are at first inclined to believe. The Saul story may be composed of materials from different origins, but the final editor must have been convinced he was presenting a story that is coherent, meaningful and enjoyable to read. Like I do with the other four biblical characters that I study in this book, I take the Saul story as we have it now, in its final form. My approach is again synchronic.

In the Samson story, Samson is the "hero" who dominates all the texts related to him. In the Lot story, however, we noticed that Lot is often presented in parallel with Abraham, so that at times the Lot story seems to be absorbed by the Abraham story. In the Saul story we find something similar: he rarely appears on his own. The first Book of Samuel opens with the prophet Samuel as the central figure (1 Samuel 1–7). Then the text moves into the institution of the monarchy and the selection of the first king. Saul becomes more of a central figure, but Samuel continues to play an important role (1 Samuel 8–15). Finally, in what follows, even though Saul remains the king, the person of David gradually takes the central position (1 Samuel 16–31). Do these last chapters belong to the Saul story or to the David story? In my book on David I have included them in the David story,[11] but since in this study we are concentrating on the person of Saul, I include them in his story. These chapters indeed belong to the two: the losing king Saul and the upcoming king David. Remarkably, Samuel has still not totally disappeared from the picture. So in what I call the Saul story, Saul appears to be absorbed first by Samuel and then later by David, but still at times appears as a figure on his own.

The life of Saul, like that of so many leaders, can be divided into three periods: the road to becoming king, his gradual disintegration, and finally his last days and death. Each of these periods of Saul's life is introduced by an encounter with the prophet Samuel. In the first encounter, Samuel announces Saul's great success (9:1–10:27). The second encounter is very disturbing: here Samuel announces the end of Saul's kingship (13:7-15). In the third encounter, Samuel announces Saul's rejection and his replacement by David (15:1–16:13), and in the last encounter Samuel announces Saul's defeat and death (28:3-25).

The texts in which Saul is presented in a positive light and which are full of hope for him are thus limited to the first part (ch. 9–14), while all the texts afterwards paint Saul in a negative light. He is described as a total failure; Saul is the failed king! He is the big loser. As we have seen before, texts that speak about losers are often written by the winners. A major change has occurred in Samuel: he chooses Saul as the first king, but ends up rejecting him. This could indicate that we find in this Saul story a prophetic perspective, probably from the northern kingdom, that wanted to stress that any disobedience to God's word proclaimed by a prophet leads to disaster. But we also notice that Saul is put aside more and more and is gradually replaced by David. Saul was from the tribe of Benjamin and thus from the North, while David was from Bethlehem of Judah and thus from the South. We may then at least suspect some political interests playing in these texts. It seems to suggest that we find in the Saul story a southern royalist perspective. It has to explain why David replaces Saul's dynasty, and to prove David's legitimacy to the throne, not only in the South but also in the North.

Because of all this political and religious maneuvring and influences, the Saul story could be a theological or a political writing, and therefore many questions could be asked about the historicity of the text. Was Saul really such a disaster historically, or was he painted as one by those who wanted to replace him while still claiming legitimacy? We could search for what happened historically. But it is not my intention to pursue this angle, or to judge Saul, as I said in the introduction to this book. Rather, I take the biblical text in its present form and try to find out why this text considers Saul a failure.

Since the Saul story is presented in so many chapters, it is impossible to go into detail and to make a close reading of all these texts. Instead, I will stress the important moments in Saul's life – his important decisions and actions. The reader could benefit greatly by keeping the biblical text close at hand and also by reading the verses or sections that I do not cover.

The Story of Saul

The Book of Judges describes the great difficulties that Israel encountered continuously with its neighbours. This was a trying time in Israel's history, as the story of Samson illustrates. Israel was in need of a political change; it needed a central authority between all the tribes so that they as one group could resist the enemy neighbours. At the time, that meant installing a king. But how can Israel have a king, since the king of Israel is the LORD? One notices the conflict between politics and religion. How can this dilemma be solved? Through the intervention of a prophet – in this case, the prophet Samuel. The struggle between the pro- and anti-monarchy tendencies, parties and arguments are well summarized in the chapter preceding the first mention of Saul (1 Samuel 8). That chapter ends with the

Lord's command to Samuel: "Obey their voice and give them a king" (v. 22).

It is important to keep this dispute in mind as we read. A person who stands at the crossroads of important changes in a society must have great leadership qualities. He must be capable of being inventive and creative: he must have the gift of finding ways to please both parties and to bring some kind of harmony in his people. A person of great understanding, but someone who can make tough decisions.

And now the story of Saul begins: "Among the men of Benjamin there was a man named Kish son of Abiel, son of Zeror, son of Becorath, son of Aphiah; a Benjaminite and a man of rank" (9:1). This Kish is obviously an important man of the northern tribe of Benjamin. He is said to be a man of rank, and his genealogical list goes back four generations. All this suggests that he must be of a family of tribal leaders. After giving the ancestors of Kish, the text adds, "he had a son named Saul, a handsome man in the prime of life. Of all the Israelites there was no one more handsome than he; he stood head and shoulders taller than the rest of the people" (v. 2). Saul, the son of Kish, possibly a tribal chief, is clearly special, and even his appearance is rather impressive. The text specifies twice that Saul is "handsome"; he is also "tall." For these two qualities Saul is compared with the rest of the people, and each time he beats them all. He is more "than" (twice) everybody else. No doubt, this young man of this important tribal family is a promising future leader.

The story opens with a banal event. One day Kish is in despair because some of his she-donkeys get lost. He sends his son Saul with a servant to try to find them. Saul, as a good son, does what his father tells him. They search everywhere but do not find the donkeys. Saul then says to his servant: "Come, let us go back or my father will stop worrying over the she-donkeys and start being anxious about us" (v. 8). This little story illustrates the fine relationship that exists between father and son; they trust each other and worry about each other. Saul is not only a handsome person; he is also a good son. The servant, however, has another proposal, and he says to Saul: "Look, there is a man of God in this town, a man held in honour; everything he says comes true. Let us go there, then; perhaps he will be able to guide us on the journey we have undertaken" (v. 6). That makes a lot of sense to Saul, which shows that he is not a dominating figure, for he accepts the advice even of a servant. His reaction also shows that he is a religious person; he believes in the importance of a man of God and he trusts God. But Saul has an objection. He says to his servant: "But if we go, what can we take to the man... What can we give him?" (v. 7). He does not use people; he wants to offer that man of God something, for such a person also needs to live. The servant luckily has a silver shekel, and that should do. Saul appears in these verses as a worthy son, a respectful master of this servant, a believer and a real gentleman in his attitude to others – in this case, towards that man of God whom he does not even know.

And now the search for the lost she-donkeys changes to a search for the man of God. While they are going through the gate of Ramah, the town of Samuel, the prophet comes out. The day before, Samuel had received a revelation from God: "About this time tomorrow I will send to you a man from the land of Benjamin; you are to anoint him as prince over my people Israel, and he will save my people from the power of the Philistines; for I have seen the distress of my people and their crying has come to me" (v. 16). The wording recalls God's decision to save Israel from slavery in Egypt by calling Moses (Exodus 3:7-10). Indeed, like the book of Judges and, above all, the story of the last judge, Samson, have shown, these Philistines are "the" danger. Israel needs more than another judge: it needs a "prince," a charismatic leader. Just as the choice of Moses as the deliverer was a divine decision, the choice of this prince is also God's work. When Samuel sees Saul, the LORD tells him: "That is the man of whom I told you; he shall rule my people" (v. 17). Here is an interesting twist to the story: Samuel has found the one chosen by God, and Saul has found Samuel the seer. Samuel tells him that the she-donkeys have been found, but then adds something remarkable: "Besides, for whom is all the wealth of Israel destined, if not for you and all your father's House?" (v. 20).

This is the first encounter between Samuel and Saul. It is a first prediction of Saul's royal destiny, but is not yet stated in very clear or explicit terms. Saul, overwhelmed by this unexpected meeting, reacts like so many people do when chosen by God for a particular mission: "Am I not a Benjaminite, from the smallest of Israel's tribes? And is not my family the least of all the families of the tribe of Benjamin? Why do you say such words?" (v. 21). One could say that this is just false humility of Saul, but then we would have to say the same thing about the reactions of Moses, Jeremiah and others. Saul truly reacts like all the great men of the Bible: he recognizes his unworthiness.

Samuel receives Saul and the servant with full honours, offering them a beautiful meal and inviting them to stay the night in the best place of the house: on the housetop. The next morning, they get up and go together with Samuel to the end of the town. There Samuel asks Saul to send his servant ahead so that they would be alone, and then adds, "and I shall make known to you the word of God" (v. 27). God had told Samuel what he had in reserve for the person he would meet; that is what Samuel now wants to tell Saul.

Samuel does not only reveal to Saul God's words, he also executes them, since God had told Samuel that he had to anoint this person. "Samuel took of phial of oil and poured it on Saul's head; then he kissed him, saying: 'Has not the LORD anointed you prince over his people Israel? You are the man who must rule the LORD's people, and who must save them from the power of the enemies surrounding them'" (10:1). Samuel's behaviour towards Saul – the way he has welcomed him and now kisses him – shows that he really likes him. To give more strength to his words, Samuel continues: "This shall be the sign for you that the LORD has appointed you prince of his heritage…" (v. 1). Prophets would frequently add a sign to their words they claim to be the word of God. The fulfillment of that sign would then be the best proof of the authenticity of that prophetic word. Samuel provides not only one but three signs; the event is indeed too important for just one. The last sign is that Saul will meet a group of prophets in ecstasy and then "the spirit of the LORD will seize on you, and you will go into an ecstasy, and be changed into another man" (vv. 1-6). Samuel adds: "When these signs are fulfilled for you, act as occasion serves, for God is with you" (v. 7).

These powerful texts say a lot about our hero. Saul, this fine gentleman, is suddenly overpowered by a prophet, who does not ask him if he is interested in the position of a new type of federal leader over the whole people of Israel. Samuel does not ask for acceptance; he simply put this charge upon Saul as being God's decision. The text is explicit: Saul did not appropriate this position by force, or by political manoeuvring, or by manipulating the religious authorities. Saul never applied for this difficult job; he even made some objections. This young man, who is such an outstanding person in the eyes of the people, is also outstanding in the eyes of God. God wants Saul and no one else, and the text adds: "for God is with you," a formula that becomes central in the life of David.

The last words of Samuel are an order: "You must go down before me to Gilgal; I will join you there to offer

SAUL: A Failed King

holocausts and communion sacrifices. You are to wait seven days for me to come to you, and then I will show you what you are to do" (v. 8). The prophet is in command; Saul has to follow the word of the prophet.

After this Saul returns home to Gibeah: "As soon as Saul had turned his back to leave Samuel, God changed his heart and all these signs were accomplished that same day" (v. 9). With the signs fulfilled, the prophet's word and action are confirmed. Samuel is a true prophet of the LORD and Saul has become the leader, for "God changed his heart." Saul, upon his return home, is glad to tell his relatives that Samuel assured him that the donkeys had been found. Understandably, "he said nothing about the kingship of which Samuel had spoken" (v. 16). Saul is not the type of person to shout from the rooftops the news of his election and his promising future. He is shy about accepting the mission entrusted to him by Samuel, and he is humble and discreet enough not to publicize the "honours" he has received. He certainly appears more humble than Joseph who liked to proclaim to everyone his dreams of his future dominion over his family, which did not make him very popular with his brothers (Genesis 37:5-11). Everything that the story has said so far about Saul is extremely positive and promising. It all hints that he will be the ideal leader that Israel needs.

Samuel has anointed Saul as leader in secret, and Saul is not publicizing it. Samuel continues to take the initiative; he assembles the people "before the LORD according to the tribes and clans" (10:19) to choose the person who is supposed to become king by lot. And "the lot fell to the tribe of Benjamin... the lot fell to the clan of Matri... the lot fell to Saul son of Kish" (vv. 20-21). This is another convincing proof that Saul's election is God's will. But Saul, the person who does not like to be in the spotlight, "was not to be found" (v. 21). The entire Saul story seems to be one of ongoing seeking and finding.

When Saul is finally found and brought to the meeting, "he stood among the people, he was head and shoulders taller than them all" (v. 23). Saul once again impresses by his physical appearance. Samuel says to the people: "Have you seen the man the LORD has chosen? Of all the people there is none to equal him" (v. 24). God has directed Samuel to find the leader for his people, and the lot has confirmed this choice. No doubt Saul is the person chosen by God, and his physical appearance confirms this. He is the leader in the eyes of God and in the eyes of the people.

The reaction of the people is unanimous; "all the people" shout with a loud voice a cry that is proclaimed for the first time in the history of Israel: "Long live the king" (v. 24). Until now, the text has spoken of Saul as a "prince" (9:16; 10:1), a leader different from the judges who came before him. Now the text clarifies what type of leader Saul will be; he is the first "king" of Israel. Saul is king not because he looked for it himself, but only because he was chosen by the LORD and by the people. The assembly is over; everyone goes home, including Saul: "he went home to Gibeah." But he does not go alone; "with him went the mighty men whose hearts God had touched" (v. 26). The new king has his own followers, the beginning of his army, all people whose hearts are deeply attached to him. But immediately after this sign of acceptance and the promise of future success follows a note that is less promising and rather surprising after the whole people has acclaimed Saul as their king: "But there were some scoundrels who said, 'How can this fellow save us?' They despised him, and offered him no present" (v. 27). Saul experiences right from the beginning what many leaders after him have experienced: acceptance and rejection, admiration and scorn. That is not easy for a leader to cope with. The text tells us how Saul reacts: "But he took no notice." This criticism does not seem to bother him; it leaves him indifferent. Saul does not only have an impressive physical appearance, but apparently he also has a strong character; he can live with opposition.

The first test of Saul as leader comes very soon. Nahash, king of the Ammonites, marches on Jabesh-gilead. The conditions he imposes on the people to come to an agreement are extremely cruel:"that I put out all your right eyes" (11:1-2). This is the moment to call upon the new leader, who "was just then coming in from the fields behind his oxen" (v. 5). Saul, even after having been anointed king and acclaimed by the people, has continued his former lifestyle. But after hearing what Nahash has in mind, he realizes that he has to act."The spirit of the LORD seized on Saul," just as when the Spirit seized on the judges (Judges 3:10; 6:34; 11:29; 14:6, 19; 15:14) and "his fury stirred to fierce flame." Here Saul reveals another aspect of his character: he can become very angry. "He took a yoke of oxen and cut them in pieces which he sent by messengers throughout the territory of Israel with these words: 'If anyone will not march with Saul, this shall be done with his oxen!'" (vv. 6-7). Saul means business. He shows that he is a strong leader. There is no time for discussion; this is the time for action. "A dread of the LORD fell on the people and they marched out as one man," and they are "three hundred thousand Israelites and thirty thousand of Judah." What no judge or any previous leader had been capable of doing, Saul does. He succeeds in bringing North and South together in the interest of the common good to rescue the people of Jabesh-gilead. Saul's victory over the Ammonites is complete: "the survivors were so scattered that not two of them were left together" (v. 11).

Saul has proven that he can motivate different tribes to become one people, and that he is a military leader capable of fighting the enemy and of saving Israel. The people then said to Samuel, "Who said: 'Is Saul to reign over us?' Hand the men over for us to put them to death" (v. 12). There were indeed those people who had despised Saul and who had said: "How can this fellow save us?" (10:27). The people feel that such troublemakers have no right to be members of this united Israel. Saul, who had not been disturbed by these scoundrels before, now comes to their rescue. "No one is to be put to death today, for today the LORD has brought victory to Israel" (v. 13). Once more we learn something of the character of Saul: he is a person who does not look for vengeance but who can forgive; he is generous, not fearful for his authority. He is also a person who knows that he himself did not bring the victory, but the LORD. Obviously Saul is not self-centred.

Samuel thereupon invites the people to go to Gilgal "to reaffirm the monarchy there," and "So all the people went to Gilgal and there they proclaimed Saul king before the LORD at Gilgal. They offered communion sacrifices there before the LORD; and Saul and all the men of Israel rejoiced greatly" (v. 15). Saul – anointed as leader by a prophet, then chosen by lot as king – has proven that indeed he is the one who is capable of saving Israel. The people, therefore, now reaffirm their acceptance. They acclaim him once more as king and celebrate, which brings great joy to Saul and to the people. Samuel has accomplished his mission: he has appointed a king who is now firmly established, and now he can give way to Saul (12:1-25).

Since Saul's mission is to save his people, it is not surprising that his next struggle is with the Philistines, "the" enemy of Israel. His oldest son, Jonathan, plays an important role in this fight. The battle that the Philistines prepare leaves no hope for Israel (13:1-7). Tragedy hits Saul's life for the first time. When Samuel anointed Saul and gave him signs to be fulfilled, he had added: "You must go down before me to Gilgal; I will join you there to offer holocausts and communion sacrifices. You are to wait seven days for me to come to you, and then I will show you what you are to do" (10:8). Saul, who is now in Gilgal, "waited for seven days, the period Samuel had fixed, but Samuel did not come to Gilgal and the army, deserting Saul, was dispersed" (v. 8). What an impossible situation for this new king! A prophet who has promised to come and does not appear, an army that deserts him and an enemy that is overpowering him! Saul knows that there is still God who can help. "So Saul said, 'Bring me the holocaust and the communion sacrifices'; and he offered the holocaust" (v. 9).

Precisely at that moment Samuel arrives and blames Saul: "What have you done?" Saul explains what seems to be a reasonable and commendable course of action: "I saw the army deserting…and you had not come at the time fixed, while the Philistines were mustering…and I had not implored the favour of the Lord. So I felt obliged to act and I offered the holocaust myself" (vv. 11-12). Samuel's reaction to Saul's very acceptable response seems far from being reasonable. He begins by accusing Saul: "You have acted as a fool." He continues by announcing the divine punishment: "If you had carried out the order the Lord your God commanded you, the Lord would have confirmed your sovereignty over Israel for ever. But now your sovereignty will not last; the Lord has searched out a man for himself after his own heart and designed him leader of his people, since you have not carried out what the Lord ordered you" (vv. 13-14). Samuel begins and ends with the same statement: the only thing that really counts is observing God's command. If Saul had done so, he would have been king forever, but since he did not, he will lose his kingship – indeed, God already has his eye on the person who will replace him. This is hard language. Samuel, in his first encounter with Saul, anointed him king. Now, in this second encounter, the prophet announces the end of his kingship.

The difficult question is this: in what way did Saul not follow God's command? He waited for Samuel to come like the prophet had asked. If Samuel was late, is Saul to blame?

Is he guilty for offering a sacrifice to God? Certainly not. On other occasions, it seems perfectly acceptable that he as king offers sacrifice (14:32-35). Is this a struggle between the religious and the secular powers in Israel? Is Samuel trying to hang on to his power? On the other hand, Samuel seems to like Saul. His accusation of Saul remains mysterious and unjustified. Is the text hiding something, like the mysterious text about Moses' sin seems to do (Numbers 20:1-13)? Or could it be simply that Samuel, realizing that he is late, wants to justify himself by blaming Saul? Prophets are not perfect; they also have their human shortcomings. Elijah, for instance, became discouraged and left his ministry (2 Kings 19). The fight between Jeremiah and Hananiah is not what one would expect from two men of God (Jeremiah 28). Jonah, as we will see in the next chapter of this book, had many faults.

After making this severe accusation, Samuel "left Gilgal" (v. 15). Even though he had told Saul that he would come and "show you what you are to do" (10:8), he does not say anything to Saul; he just leaves him with this incomprehensible condemnation that suggests a profound break. The new king is left to himself. The text does not say anything about what goes on in Saul's heart. He does not react; he does not ask for explanations from Samuel. Earlier, it had not disturbed him that some people despised him (10:27). Was he also able to set aside these hard words of Samuel? In any case, they have not totally broken Saul's sense of duty. He is the king, responsible for his people who are in danger because of the Philistines, and so "Saul went to join the warriors… he inspected the force…" (v. 15). We as readers can only guess what this second encounter signifies for Saul, but it is hard to believe that it left him indifferent.

Jonathan, Saul's eldest son, gets deeply involved in the battle against the Philistines (14:1-17). When Saul sees how the people panic, he says to the priest Ahijah, "Bring the ephod" (v. 18). The king knows that the victory is not his, but in the hands of God, as he had confessed after his first victory over the Ammonites (11:13). He therefore wants to consult the LORD before joining the battle. "But while he was speaking to the priest, the turmoil in the Philistine camp grew worse and worse." Now Saul does something strange. He says to the priest, "Withdraw your hand" (v. 19). While the priest is ready to draw the lots, Saul stops him and goes straight to the battlefield without waiting for the divine oracle. Is Saul a person who lacks patience and is always in a hurry? Could that explain what happened when Samuel did not arrive after seven days? Samuel arrived just as Saul started the sacrifices. If Saul had waited just a few more minutes, there would have been no problem! But this time Saul is not blamed for his actions at all. On the contrary, "that day the LORD gave Israel the victory…" (v. 23).

Saul, besides wanting to consult the LORD before going to battle, did something more to obtain the LORD's favour: "Saul had imposed a great fast that day, laying the people under an oath, 'Cursed be the man who eats food before evening, before I have had my revenge on my enemies!'" (v. 24). He even built an altar to the LORD (v. 35). But again misfortune hits Saul. Jonathan, who had not heard his father's decision, eats a little honeycomb. Later in the day, Saul consults God once more to see if he should continue to pursue the Philistines, but gets no answer. The king thus realizes that someone must have sinned against the LORD. The lot is cast between Saul and Jonathan on one side and the people on the other side. The lot indicates first that the fault lies with Saul and Jonathan, and then the lot decides that Jonathan is the guilty one.

Saul is in a terrible dilemma; he has made an oath before God and now discovers his son's unintentional transgression. Jonathan declares himself ready to die, and so Saul declares before the whole people: "May God do this to me and more if you do not die, Jonathan" (v. 44). Saul is in a similar situation to Abraham, who also believed that God asked him to sacrifice his son (Genesis 22), and to Jephthah, who made a vow that cost the life of his daughter (Judges 11:29-40). How cruel it all seems: Saul shows that his love for the LORD is more important and transcends his love for his son. What he has promised to God cannot be changed. Saul proves to be a person of principles, which of course makes the blame Samuel placed on him seem even more strange and incomprehensible. The king is ready to offer his son, but the people ransom Jonathan, probably to the great relief of his father.

A short but important paragraph in the Saul story summarizes the king's military successes. It also presents Saul's blessed family; with his wife Ahinoam they have three sons and two daughters. Finally, it describes how Saul installs his administration and builds up his professional army (14:47-52). Saul, the first king of Israel, seems to succeed in giving Israel what it needs as a leader. The first part of the Saul story (ch. 9–14) thus presents the positive side of his career. However, Samuel's words are already there in the shadows, throwing some darkness over this beautiful picture. Saul will not be king forever; he will not form a dynasty.

From now on, after this successful beginning, things go downhill. It all starts with a third encounter between Samuel and Saul. The prophet had once promised the king that he would tell him what to do (10:8). This seems to be the moment for it. Samuel invites Saul "to listen to the words of the LORD," and the divine message is: "…to strike down Amalek; put him under the ban with all that he possesses. Do not spare him…" (15:1-3). This is a call to "Holy"War. And that means that since the LORD gives the victory to Israel, all the enemies and their belongings have to be sacrificed to him. This cruel behaviour, also practised by other peoples at the time, had somehow a religious meaning. People had no right to enrich themselves by war. Everything had to be given to God (Deuteronomy 13:17; 20:16–18).

Saul accepts the divine command to go to war; he summons the people and defeats the Amalekites. "He took Agag king of the Amalekites alive and, executing the ban, put all the people to the sword." (vv. 4–8). Everything seems to be in order; there is, however, a "but." "But Saul and the army spared Agag with the best of the sheep and cattle, the fatlings and lambs and all that was good. They did not want to put those under the ban; they only put under the ban what was poor and worthless" (v. 9). This time the text shows clearly that Saul does not observe the divine order that the prophet gave him. We cannot use the excuse that Saul could not force himself to kill and that he has too much compassion. He has no scruples about killing and carrying out the ban; he does it, but only in part. He is selective. He and his army keep the best for themselves.

There are no secrets from God, and so "The word of the LORD came to Samuel, 'I regret having made Saul king, for he has turned away from me and has not carried out my orders" (v. 10). The first time, we may have wondered what Saul had done wrong, how he had not obeyed God's commands (13:13–15). This time it is clear what Saul has done wrong, and how he has not obeyed God's commands. But now it is Samuel who "was deeply moved, and all night long he cried out to the LORD" (v. 11). Samuel feels deeply for Saul. Rather than seeing him as a threat to his own authority, he is hurt and disappointed. The person he had trusted has misled him!

Samuel goes to meet Saul, and Saul says to him: "Blessed may you be by the LORD! I carried out the LORD's orders" (v. 13). Saul and his people have been shown to be greedy, and now he proves that he is dishonest; he tries to hide his fault with lies. But how can he hide the truth when Samuel hears the bleating of sheep and the lowing of oxen? Saul, however, has his answer ready: he and his army have spared the best "to sacrifice them to the LORD, your God." This answer is not acceptable to Samuel, who accuses Saul of disobedience to the LORD. Saul continues to maintain that he really did obey God, since he intended to sacrifice what he had spared. He also adds another detail, common to human nature: after he tries unsuccessfully to hide, he blames others: "From the booty the people took the best…" This is a poor excuse; a leader must be able to control his people. A king must obey only God, and not give in to the desires of his people (vv. 14-21). But it may well be that Saul was indeed honest. It is possible that he and the people had spared the best to sacrifice it to the LORD. If so, then there is not much difference between putting everything under the ban or sacrificing it as an offering. Is Saul honest or is he lying and trying to cover it up? For Samuel there is no hesitation; obeying the voice of the LORD is more important than sacrifices (vv. 22-23a). In other words, Saul has to obey the LORD the way God wants, not the way Saul wants. Samuel concludes: "Since you have rejected the word of the LORD, he has rejected you as king" (v. 23b). He cannot speak plainer on this issue. This time, Saul must understand why, even if the punishment seems disproportionate.

Saul's reaction again shows his positive side. He stops making excuses, accepts his fault and confesses it: "I have sinned, for I have transgressed the order of the LORD… Now I pray, forgive my sin; come back with me and I will worship the LORD" (vv. 24-25). But his confession and request are not accepted. Samuel's refusal is as mysterious as his first accusation (13:13-15). If we compare Samuel's reaction with what happens to Saul's successor, David, Samuel's refusal becomes even more questionable. David also sins, and after a prophet challenges him, has the courage to say, "I have sinned." But to him the prophet Nathan declared: "the LORD forgives your sin" (2 Samuel 12:13-14). Why did Saul not find this same mercy?

Perhaps we can explain the difference by examining more closely the two situations. The penalty for David's sin was death; Nathan forgives him, adding: "you are not to die." That does not mean that David will not be punished, however. The punishment for Saul's disobedience is not death, but the loss of his kingship, his authority and thus his prestige. Saul's life is not in danger. He can go on living – albeit in a humbled condition. It is interesting that Samuel makes reference to this when he says to Saul: "Small as you may be in your own eyes, are you not head of the tribes of Israel?" (v. 17). Saul had confessed his humble and "small" origins (9:21), but God had still chosen him as king. Now that Saul has failed as a leader, he will become small: not only in his own eyes, but in the eyes of the people. But still, this refusal of mercy is hard to understand.

When Samuel tries to leave, Saul in a last effort "caught at the hem of his garment and it tore." Samuel sees in this accident a sign: "Today the LORD has torn the kingdom of Israel from you and given it to a neighbour of yours who is better than you" (vv. 27-28). Saul once more confesses, "I have sinned"; he no longer asks to be forgiven, since forgiveness has been refused to him. Now he has another request: "but please still show me respect in front of the elders of my people and in front of Israel, and come back with me, so that I can worship the LORD your God" (v. 30). Note that Saul always says "your God" and not "our God." He realizes that the LORD has rejected him, but still hopes for some respect from his people. He is afraid to lose face. Samuel grants him this last request at least.

Samuel returns to his hometown, Ramah, and Saul to his town, Gibeah. The text ends this third encounter by revealing something to the reader: "Samuel did not see Saul again to the day of his death; Samuel was very sorry for Saul, but the LORD regretted having made Saul king of Israel" (v. 35). Why this tragic end to a beautiful and deep relationship? If Samuel feels sorry, why can he not forgive? If the LORD regrets, why can he too not forgive? Saul is now on his own.

It is not easy for Samuel to be a friend to Saul and at the same time to play the role of a prophet. The LORD then says to Samuel: "How long will you go on mourning over Saul when I have rejected him as king of Israel? Fill your horn with oil and go. I am sending you to Jesse of Bethlehem, for I have chosen myself a king among his sons" (16:1). Samuel objects: "How can I go? When Saul hears of it he will kill me" (v. 2). Samuel says this, perhaps as an excuse, but we do not know if indeed Saul would do this. Saul has proven himself to be someone who does not seem threatened by opposition (10:27; 11:12-13) but he can get angry and requires obedience to his orders (11:6-7). We will have to wait and see how Saul reacts to the person who gradually seems to take over as future king. Samuel follows the divine command and in secret anoints David, the son of Jesse of Bethlehem, as the new king (16:1-13). We as readers are told this story, but Saul is not. Samuel had also anointed him as king in secret, but then there was no other king. This time things are different. While Saul is still king in the eyes in the people, but not in the eyes of God, there is now another king in the eyes of God, but not yet in the eyes of the people.[12]

When Samuel broke with Saul after telling him that the LORD had rejected him as king and that his kingdom would be given to a neighbour of his (15:23-28), we could only guess what was going on in Saul's heart. Now, after the secret anointing of David, the narrator gives us some information: "Now the spirit of the LORD had left Saul" (v. 14a). We know what the spirit of the LORD does to any leader of Israel, such as the judges, and what he did to Saul himself (11:6). The spirit gives strength, courage, and enthusiasm to fight and conquer the enemy. That is over for

Saul; he lacks what any leader needs. That in itself would be disastrous, but the text adds: "and an evil spirit of the LORD filled him with terror" (v. 14b). On top of losing what he needs to be a leader, Saul is filled with the opposite. Instead of strength and courage, he is filled with fear and terror; instead of enthusiasm, he moves into depression.

Saul's servants notice the tremendous change in the king and they care for him: "Let our lord give the order, and your servants who wait on you will look for a skilled harpist; when the evil spirit of God troubles, the harpist will play and you will recover" (v. 16). Saul agrees; he wants to recover his inner peace. As luck would have it, the best harpist found is David, so Saul asks Jesse to send him his son David. It is friendship at first sight: "David came to Saul and entered his service; Saul loved him greatly" (v. 21). David is very successful in helping the king; "whenever the spirit from God troubled Saul, David took the harp and played; then Saul grew calm, and recovered, and the evil spirit left him" (v. 23). The evil spirit may leave Saul, but it is never said that the spirit of the LORD returns to Saul; he never recovers his enthusiasm and his courage.

That courage to fight is what Saul now needs in the battle against the Philistines, who muster their troops for war while Saul does the same (17:1–3). The Philistine giant Goliath proposes a single combat with one man of Israel instead of a battle between the two armies. "When Saul and all Israel heard these words of the Philistine they were dismayed and terrified" (v. 11). Saul has lost all stamina one would expect from a king; he offers instead a good reward for the person who would dare to accept. "The king will lavish riches on the man who kills him and give him his daughter in marriage and grant his father's House the freedom of Israel" (v. 25). David presents himself. Saul objects at first, saying "you are only a boy" (v. 33), but finally accepts: "Go, and the LORD be with you" (v. 37). Saul, who no longer has the spirit of the LORD upon himself, expresses a wish for David – a wish for which he does not realize or foresee the deep implications. Indeed, God is with David, who kills Goliath. From now on God will be with David.

After this exceptional victory, David is given a special place in Saul's home: "Saul kept him by him from that day forward and would not let him go back to his father's house" (18:2). When Saul met David first as a harpist, Saul "loved David greatly" (16:21). After his military exploits, it is Jonathan, Saul's eldest son, who feels deeply for David: "he came to love him as his own soul" (18:1, 3). Saul puts David in charge of the military. David is very successful and so he "stood well in the people's eyes and in the eyes of Saul's officers" (v. 5). Saul had said to David: "the LORD will be with you," and that is now happening more and more.

One day everything changes. To celebrate David's victory the women come out to meet Saul and they sing: "Saul has killed his thousands, and David his ten thousands" (v. 7). Saul may be a handsome man (9:2), but he is getting older. David is also very handsome (16:12), but younger, and is now a military hero. He gets the attention of the singing and dancing women. That is too much for Saul. "Saul was very angry; the incident was not to his liking. 'They have given David the tens of thousands,' he said 'but me only the thousands; he has all but the kingship now'" (v. 8). Saul does not realize how true his words are; David is already anointed as king. "And Saul turned a jealous eye on David from that day forward" (v. 9). This is another important turning point in Saul's life, with consequences that match those of his rejection by Samuel.

It does not take long to see that Saul has become a totally different person: "On the following day an evil spirit from God seized on Saul and he fell into a fit of frenzy while he was in his house. David was playing the harp as on other days" (v. 10). This had become a usual scene in the royal house, but something has changed. "Saul had his spear in his hand. Saul brandished the spear; 'I am going to pin David to the wall,' he said" (v. 11). Samuel had been right (16:2). Saul is capable of killing a person whom he sees as a threat, but "David twice evaded him." Saul tries twice without success. Nothing seems to work for Saul anymore, while everything that David tries turns out for the best. And so "Saul feared David" (v. 12), and "Saul was frightened of him" (v. 15). We now know what is going on in Saul's heart: love for David has changed through jealousy into fear.

The only way out that Saul sees is to make sure that David disappears. He tried to kill him with his spear, but that did not work. So he finds another trick that other leaders have used. Saul had promised that the person who would kill Goliath would have his daughter to marry. He thus says to David, "Here is my elder daughter Merab; I will give her to you in marriage." That is the right thing to do, but Saul invents a new condition: "but you must serve me bravely and fight the battles of the LORD" (v. 17). It is easy to guess what Saul's real intentions are: "Let it be not my hand that strikes him down, but the hand of the Philistines." Saul starts a double game; he does not respect any rules anymore. Instead of giving Merab as wife to David, he gives her to another person (v. 19).

But the more people complicate life for others, the more life becomes complicated for themselves. Michal, Saul's second daughter, falls in love with David (18:20). Saul, far from being disturbed by this, sees in it another chance to trick David. He promises to give David his daughter on condition that David would bring him a hundred foreskins of the Philistines. Saul is convinced that David will fall into the hands of the Philistines. But that is not at all how things develop, and so Saul is obliged to give his daughter to David, who thus becomes Saul's son-in-law.

The facts speak for themselves to Saul: "he realized that the LORD was with David, and that all the house of Israel loved him" and consequently "Saul feared David all the more and became David's lasting enemy" (v. 28). Once more we peer into the heart of Saul and discover deep fear. Saul does not fear for his life, for David has never shown any sign that he would like to kill him, but Saul is afraid to lose his kingship and thus his authority and prestige (see 18:8). To avoid that at all cost, Saul sees only one solution: the death of David. He has tried with his own spear, but David escaped. Saul then tried to engineer David's death by sending him to extremely dangerous military missions, but David always comes back safe, "every time... David was more successful than all Saul's officers" (v. 30). David's success increases and Saul's fear increases proportionately!

Saul then tries another strategy. "Saul told Jonathan his son and all his servants of his intention to kill David" (19:1). By including his eldest son and his trusted servants in his plans, Saul hopes to succeed in killing his enemy. A father should be able to rely on his eldest son, the person who normally would become king after his father's death. Jonathan would therefore also gain by the disappearance of David, who clearly had become a threat to his right of succession. But again Saul is not lucky. Everything seems to work against him. "Now Jonathan, Saul's son, held David in great affection; and so Jonathan warned David" (v. 2). Another of Saul's projects does not work! Jonathan even succeeds in convincing his father: "Why then sin against innocent blood in killing David without cause?" (v. 5) Saul takes an oath not to kill David: "As the LORD lives, I will not kill him" (v. 6). Reconciliation is done, and "David attended on him as before" (v. 7). Peace has been restored, but not for long.

Life repeats itself. David once again is very successful in a battle against the Philistines, and of course jealousy re-

SAUL: A Failed King

enters Saul's heart. "An evil spirit from the LORD came on Saul while he was sitting in his house with his spear in his hand; David was playing the harp. Saul tried to pin David to the wall with his spear, but he avoided Saul's thrust and the spear stuck in the wall" (vv. 9-10). This begins to sound familiar. Nothing seems to halt Saul's firm decision to kill David, not even his oath in the name of the LORD. David also realizes that Saul is determined, so he escapes.

But of course a king has his secret agents: "That same night Saul sent agents to watch David's house, intending to kill him in the morning" (v. 11). This time David's wife Michal, Saul's daughter, finds ways to help her husband to escape. Saul did not have help from his eldest son; neither does he get any from his daughter. Both his children take David's side against their father. Saul blames her: "Why have you deceived me like this and let my enemy go, and so make his escape?" (v. 17). Is there anyone left whom Saul can count on?

David tried to escape from Saul's house to his own house, but he is no longer safe there either, so he decides to seek refuge with Samuel in Ramah (v. 18). After all, the prophet is the cause of his present troubles; he had anointed David in secret. Saul finds out where he is and sends agents to capture David there, but "the spirit of God came on Saul's agents, and they fell into an ecstasy" (v. 20). They lose all their power and fail to capture David. Saul sends a second group with the same result, and then a third, and they too fall into ecstasy. Saul then makes what must be a difficult decision: he goes to see Samuel. Their last encounter had been a disaster. Samuel had totally rejected him, and all that has happened since seems to confirm that indeed God is no longer with Saul. The narrator even said that Samuel never saw Saul again to the day of his death (15:35).

Saul risks going to Samuel's house, but what had happened with his agents, happens to him: "the spirit of

God came on him too" (v. 23). The spirit of God, which used to come upon Saul as a leader but had left him a long time ago, returns to him for just one moment. This spirit is not the one that gives courage and strength to the leader of Israel, but a spirit that puts him into ecstasy: "He too stripped off his clothes and he too fell into ecstasy in the presence of Samuel, and falling down lay there naked all that day and night" (v. 24). Not one word is said between Samuel and Saul. Saul lies there in the presence of the prophet − naked and powerless without his spear. Meanwhile, David escapes unhurt.

David, always on the run, tries another way of escape. Saul had tried to use Jonathan to kill David (19:1); now David tries to use Jonathan to escape from Saul (20:1). The two invent a complicated plan to discover if Saul has really decided to kill David. Saul becomes aware that things are not right and he insults his son: "You son of a wanton! Do I not know that you are in league with the son of Jesse to your own disgrace and the disgrace of your mother's nakedness? As long as the son of Jesse lives on the earth neither your person nor your royal rights are secure. Now, send and bring him to me; he is condemned to death" (vv. 30-31). Jonathan tries once more to appease his father: "Why should he die? What has he done?" Saul does not give an answer, but takes action: "Saul brandished his spear at him to strike him down, and Jonathan knew then that his father had already made up his mind that David should die" (v. 33). Saul had once nearly sacrificed his son Jonathan, who then had been ransomed by the people, probably to his father's great relief (14:43-45). Fear and anger are overpowering Saul more and more; he is even ready to kill his own son. When Jonathan tells David of this development, he realizes that there is no going back. His only chance for survival is to leave.

David had gone to the prophet Samuel; now he goes to Ahimelech the priest of Nob, who receives him very well, but Doeg, one of Saul's servants, happens to be there and witnesses this visit (21:2-10). From there, David decides to seek refuge in Gath by the Philistines (vv. 11-16), then goes to Adullam, and so on, from place to place (22:1-5). He does not feel safe anywhere. He has become a wanderer from one hiding place to another to escape Saul.

Saul, of course, through his information system "came to hear that David and the men with him had been discovered." The king plans a general meeting in his city of Gibeah, "spear in the hand, with his officers standing around him" (v. 6). His words to these officers reveal how Saul feels these days: "you all conspire against me. No one told me when my son made a pact with the son of Jesse; none of you felt sorry for me or told me when my son incited my servant to become my enemy" (vv. 7-8). Saul feels abandoned by everyone: by David, by his own son, and now by his officers. He suggests that nobody feels sorry for him; he is full of self-pity. A leader who has such feelings can become extremely dangerous.

Saul finds at least one person who takes his side, but he is a foreigner! Doeg, an Edomite who witnessed how the priest of Nob generously received David on his flight from Saul (see 21:2-10) stands up and tells the whole story. Saul's anger increases, as does his determination to kill not only David but also those who help him. Saul had been ready to kill his own son, Jonathan, for speaking in favour of David. Now Saul turns his anger to the priest of Nob, whom he convokes at his home. Saul plays the roles of victim, accuser and judge. He accuses the priest: "Why have you conspired against me?" (v. 13). Saul had accused his officers of conspiring against him; he now accuses the priest of the same crime. To do anything for David is a conspiracy against Saul. The priest is surprised to be so accused and claims "to know nothing whatever of the whole affair" (v. 15).

This excuse is unacceptable to Saul. Without any further investigation or possibility for the priest to defend himself, Saul declares the death penalty not only for the priest but also for his whole house. Saul is making things terrible for himself. The spirit of God has already left him; killing the priests of God is not going to help him to regain that divine spirit. Saul orders his guardsmen: "Step forward and put the priests of the LORD to death, for they too supported David, they knew he was making his escape yet did not tell me" (v. 17).

And now a terrible thing happens to Saul. He is a king whose orders are no longer followed: his own guardsmen refuse to execute his orders because they "would not lift a hand to strike the priests of the LORD" (v. 17). One does not touch the ministers of God. But Doeg, the foreigner, has no such scruples; he kills the priest. Perhaps he will get a promotion at Saul's house! But Saul's anger is not appeased by the priest's death. "As for Nob, the town of the priests, Saul put it to the sword, men and women, children and infants, cattle and donkeys and sheep" (v. 19). His behaviour has become totally irresponsible and even incomprehensible. Saul had refused to execute the ban in his war against the Amalekites, which was why Samuel and the LORD rejected him (15:1-23). Now Saul seems to execute a ban on Nob, a city of his own people – and not any ordinary city, but the city of the priests. Is Saul trying to take his revenge against God? His action isolates him even more. How will he be able to consult the LORD now? Saul is burning his own bridges behind him.

David continues to be on the run from one place to another. Saul follows, not giving David any chance to escape. David next stop is at Keilah (23:1-6). When Saul hears this, he is certain: "God has delivered him into my power, for he has walked into a trap by going into a town with gates and bars" (v. 7). But how can Saul be so sure that God could still be on his side? Of course that is not the case. Saul is wrong: "God did not deliver him into his power" (v. 14) and David escapes. God may not be on Saul's side, but the king still has a few people on his side. Some men of Ziph tell him that David is hiding among them, and they promise: "it will be our task to deliver him into the king's power" (v. 20). Saul must have felt good and uplifted; he still has a few friends. Saul almost captures David, but the pursuit is interrupted by very bad news brought to him by a messenger: "Come at once, the Philistines have invaded the country" (v. 27). Saul does something that is to his honour: "Saul broke off his pursuit of David and went to fight the Philistines" (v. 28). Despite all his anger against David and his firm desire to get rid of him, Saul puts his people first. He cannot let them fall into the hands of the Philistines, the enemy of Israel. After showing the negative side of his character, he again shows his positive side, which was so prevalent at the beginning of his career. Saul keeps some human dignity.

This is, however, just a short respite for David; after pursuing the Philistines, Saul returns to what has become his main project in life. He learns that David is now in the wilderness of Engedi (24:1-2). After his previous failures, Saul takes all possible measures to make sure that this time he will get David: "Saul took three thousand men chosen from the whole of Israel and went in search of David" (v. 3). Such a large number of men should do! But Saul, like any other human being, goes to relieve himself in one of the caves. And what a coincidence! Is it bad luck, fate or divine providence? David and his men are hiding in that same cave. Now the roles are reversed. In the previous story Saul was strong and David vulnerable (23:26); now David is in a position of strength and the king is at his mercy. David's men see the chance of a lifetime. They encourage David: "Today is the day of which the LORD said to you, 'I will deliver your enemy into your power, do what you like with him'" (v. 5). David refuses to kill "the anointed of the LORD" (v. 7), but without being noticed he succeeds in cutting off the border of Saul's cloak. Saul, unaware that anything has happened, leaves the cave, but David calls after him. With the piece of cloak in his hand, David has visible proof that he could have killed Saul. He has no bad intentions against the king; Saul is the one who imagines that David is a threat to him.

Saul's reaction is moving. He asks: "Is that your voice, my son David?" (v. 17). Saul loved David from the first moment they met; he took him into his own house and treated him like a son. David became Saul's son-in-law. And yet all that has changed now that Saul sees David as a danger to his own position. From being like Saul's son, David has become his worst enemy. And now "Saul wept aloud" (v. 17). In Saul's heart are fear, jealousy, anger and hatred, but also love and regret. Saul makes a most sincere confession (vv. 18-22). He begins by singing David's praises and admitting his own sinfulness: "You are a more upright man than I, for you have repaid me with good while I have repaid you with evil. Today you have crowned your goodness towards me since the LORD had put me in your power yet you did not kill me. When a man comes on his enemy, does he let him go unmolested?" Saul prays that God will reward David and now openly admits what he has feared for so long: that David will be the future king: "May the LORD reward you for the goodness you have shown today. Now I know you will indeed reign and that the sovereignty in Israel will be secure in your hands." What Saul has feared and what has pushed him to try to kill David now appears to him as evident, and even as a good thing. David will be the right king for Israel. Saul ends his confession with a request: "Now swear to me by the LORD that you will not cut off my descendants after me nor blot out my name from my family." And that David swears.

It appears that peace has been restored, and that the two antagonists accept to live with a new reality, but David's actions suggest that he continues to have his suspicions. Saul "went home," which is the normal and natural thing for him to do. But "David and his men with him went back to the stronghold" (v. 23). Why does David not accompany Saul to Gibeah? Why does he return to his stronghold? Does David not trust Saul? Does he wonder about the sincerity of the king's conversion? Or has he decided that the time has come for him to go his own way? Whatever the reason, David's attitude is not very encouraging for Saul; after this humiliating step of confession, David does not offer a gesture of reconciliation.

After a short note on the death of Samuel (25:1), the Saul story and the David story begin all over again. History repeats itself. David continues his wandering, moving to Maon (25:2-44). The men of Ziph, who informed Saul of David's hiding place before (23:19), once more tell the king David's whereabouts (26:1). Saul, with the same "three thousand men" he had taken to go to Engedi (24:3), goes now "to search for David in the wilderness of Ziph" (v. 2). Saul's conversion apparently did not last long; his tears of sorrow and guilt have dried. We may at least wonder, however, if things might have been different if David had agreed to return with Saul after Saul had admitted his mistake. But this did not happen and Saul falls back into his old pattern of fear, jealousy and hatred. David must thus have been reaffirmed that his suspicions had been valid. Just as Saul discovered where David was, so David finds out that Saul is pursuing him, that he has arrived and where he is camping. In the dark, David and some of his men approach Saul's camp "where they found Saul lying asleep inside the camp, his spear stuck in the ground beside his head" (v. 7). David has his second chance, as his confidant tells him: "Today God has put your enemy in your power" (v. 8). Once again, David refuses to touch the anointed of the LORD. But "he took the spear and the pitcher of water from beside Saul's head, and they made off" (v. 12).

Saul is a lost man; he is without his spear, which he had always ready to kill David, and without water he has no chance to survive in the desert. David, from the top of the mountain, calls to the camp of Saul; the spear and the pitcher of water are the sign that he could have killed the sleeping Saul easily.

Saul reacts like he did the first time: "Is that your voice, my son David?" (v. 17). Once again he addresses David as his son. Saul does not weep this time, but this confession is stronger than the first one. He begins by honestly accepting his fault: "I have sinned." He repeats the exact same words he said after Samuel accused him of disobeying God's orders (15:24). After this admission of guilt Saul moves to a request: "Come back, my son David." This request also resembles his request to Samuel (15:25, 30). Saul invites David to return to the royal palace that he had left (19:11-12). There is no reason for David to go to a foreign land (vv. 19-20), and to this request Saul adds a promise: "I will never harm you again," for the reason that "you have shown such respect for my life today." David has respected the life of Saul, who now promises to do the same for David. He concludes his confession with the same idea he expressed in the beginning. He admits that he was wrong: "Yes, my course has been folly and my error grave" (v. 21). After David's reply, Saul ends again with a prayer that God might bless David for his generosity: "May you be blessed, my son." This is the third time that he calls David his son. And as in the first confession, Saul foresees and admits the success of David's future: "You will do great things and will succeed" (v. 25).

Is this Saul's real, permanent conversion after his first one, which did not hold for long? Once again, David's actions suggest that he is not convinced and that he continues to have his suspicions. Saul naturally "returned home" again, and David "went on his way" (v. 25). He does exactly like the first time; he clearly distrusts Saul.

SAUL: A Failed King

Once more it is a very sad situation for Saul. He has again accepted the blame, he has begged David to come home with him, but David rejects that offer; he does not respond to Saul's reaching out to him. This is the last time that Saul and David meet, and their encounter ends with a complete separation between the two men, former friends who are now enemies.

That David does not trust the repenting Saul is clear to the reader, who is given a window on David's thoughts. "'One of these days,' David thought, 'I shall perish at the hand of Saul'" (27:1a). Who knows if David's thinking is right or wrong, but David does not give Saul a chance. David continues his flight, but this time he makes a drastic decision: "I can do no better than escape to the land of the Philistines; then Saul will give up tracking me…and I will be safe from him" (v. 1b). David becomes a traitor, joining the camp of "the" enemy.

These dangerous Philistines once more "mustered their forces for war to fight Israel" (28:1), they "pitched camp at Shunem" and "Saul mustered all Israel and they camped at Giboa" (v. 4). The narrator reveals once more what goes on in Saul's heart: "When Saul saw the Philistine camp he was afraid and there was a great trembling in his heart" (v. 5). We have often been informed of Saul's fear and the fear of his troops in front of the Philistines (13:6-7; 14:15; 17:11), but now the text stresses that Saul is extremely fearful (vv. 5, 15, 20, 21). Whenever Saul has tried to obtain God's help, he has failed. The first time he implored God with a sacrifice, for which he was blamed and rejected by Samuel (15:8-15). The next time Saul tried to consult God through the priest Ahijah and the ephod, but that did not work out either (14:18-19); Saul even imposed a great fast laying the people under an oath (14:24). The LORD had then given Saul the victory, but at the same time disaster had hit him when Jonathan unconsciously broke the oath. Now Saul is once again facing the Philistines. As usual, "Saul consulted the LORD," but the story follows the same pattern. "The LORD gave him no answer, either by dream or oracle or prophet" (v. 6). Samuel, the prophet is dead (v. 3), and even if he were still alive he had separated himself from Saul. The king had massacred the priests so he cannot consult them either. And the spirit of the LORD had left him; worse, an evil spirit had come over him, so Saul's dreams do not give him insights but inspire in him fear and anguish. Saul is at a terrible impasse. He knows that he needs to consult the divinity. But what possibility is left? All legitimate ways are closed for Saul; he is completely isolated.

Saul says to his servants: "Find a woman who is a necromancer for me to go and consult her" (v. 7).[13] He knows that this is against the divine law (Leviticus 19:31). In his religious zeal he even tried to implement this law very strictly when he as king "had expelled the necromancers and wizards from the country" (v. 3). Here he acts not only against the law, but also against his own religious reforms. Apparently, however, he had not succeeded in expelling them all, since there is still one living at En-dor. And "so Saul, disguising himself and changing his clothes, set out accompanied by two men; their visit to the woman took place at night" (v. 8). Obviously the king is ill at ease and wants the whole affair to remain secret, but he sees this illegitimate way of consulting the divinity as his last resort. He asks the woman: "Disclose the future to me by means of a ghost. Conjure up the one I shall name to you" (v. 8). The woman, not suspecting that she is talking to Saul, objects. She fears that if the king, who expelled the necromancers, hears about her, he will kill her. This suggests that Saul used radical means to get rid of them, as he did with the priests of Nob. Saul reassures the woman and even swears to her: "As the LORD lives, no blame shall attach to you for this business" (v. 10). The story is getting worse and worse: Saul going against the law of the LORD, reassures this woman by the LORD. The woman accepts and asks Saul: "Whom shall I conjure up for you?" Saul's answer defies all expectation; it seems absurd. He asks her, "Conjure up Samuel" (v. 11).

There were three previous major encounters between Saul and Samuel. The first was extremely promising, as Samuel had anointed Saul king and predicted a bright future for him (9:11–10:16). The second was disturbing for Saul, for Samuel rebuked him for disobeying God and announced the end of his kingship (13:7-15). The third confirmed this more strongly (15:1-31). Samuel had then rejected Saul as king; Saul begged Samuel to return, but the prophet refused. The two had separated without seeing each other ever again. Now Saul, who does not get any divine answer by the accepted ways for consulting God, tries a forbidden means to consult the ghost of a dead person. And he chooses Samuel, of all people! If Samuel has already rejected Saul and refused to come back to him, will he now come back through this unacceptable practice? Saul is clearly desperate; perhaps he is counting on his earlier good relationship and friendship with Samuel. Or maybe Samuel, after his death, has softened his attitude towards Saul. Saul must have thought it worth a try.

And, surprisingly, Samuel comes back this time. This, then, is the fourth major encounter between Samuel and Saul. After the woman describes what she sees, "Saul knew it was Samuel and he bowed down his face to the ground and did homage" (v. 14). Saul must have been grateful that Samuel came; he shows him all his respect. But Samuel is less excited; he wonders why Saul has disturbed his rest. The reader knows the answer to that question. Saul reveals it to Samuel now: "I am in great distress; the Philistines are waging war against me, and God has abandoned me and no longer answers me either by prophet or dream; and so I have summoned you to tell me what I must do" (v. 15). Saul is extremely honest; he does not hide anything. He is afraid not only for himself, but for his people, and God does not answer, leaving him and thus also his people at the mercy of the Philistines. Saul tells Samuel that he is the only one who can still help him and his people.

Samuel's answer is hard and painful: "And why do you consult me, when the LORD has abandoned you and is with your neighbour? The LORD has done to you as he foretold through me; he has snatched the sovereignty from your hand and given it to your neighbour, David, because you disobeyed the voice of the LORD and did not execute his fierce anger against Amalek. That is why the LORD treats you like this" (vv. 16-18). This first part of Samuel's answer is a reminder of what he said to Saul in the third encounter (15:10-31). He refers once more to the disobedience of Saul, the reason why the LORD has rejected him as king and intends to give his kingship to Saul's "neighbour" (twice). This is the term Samuel used in the previous encounter (15:28), but he is now more explicit and he names that neighbour: David. That must have sounded like sacrilege in Saul's ears. The LORD is going to give the throne to the person who, like a traitor, has joined the Philistines who are now waging war on Israel and its king. But Samuel does not stop with a reminder of his previous message. He continues, "What is more, the LORD will deliver Israel and you, too, into the power of the Philistines. Tomorrow you and your sons will be with me; and Israel's army, too, for the LORD will deliver it into the power of the Philistines" (v. 19). Saul desperately tried to find out God's answer; the second part of Samuel's speech answers Saul's quest, but it is devastating news. In the third encounter, Samuel had announced that Saul is rejected as king. In this fourth and final encounter[In the third encounter,] Samuel had announced Saul's defeat and death – not in an undisclosed future but for "tomorrow."

These are Samuel's last words. After uttering them he disappears for good from the scene, leaving Saul with this cruel message. Saul's reaction does not surprise us: "Saul was overcome and fell full-length on the ground. He was terrified by what Samuel had said and, besides this, he was weakened by having eaten nothing at all that day and all that night" (v. 20). Like Saul had done in the past (14:24), he must have imposed upon himself a fast to show God his goodwill. The only person who seems to care about this rejected king is the necromancer, who offers him some food. She may have been practising something that was not accepted by the divine law, but she has a good heart and cares for this person who had come to her disguised and full of fear and who is now so terrified that he cannot move. The king refuses, saying, "I will not eat" (v. 23). How can he break his fast? But the woman and Saul's servants insist, and the king accepts. The meal she prepares for this crushed Saul is a royal meal. Samuel had offered Saul his first royal meal (9:22-24); this necromancer offers him his last one. The contrast is striking. "After they had eaten they set off and left that same night" (v. 25). And there goes Saul into the night knowing that he is moving towards his defeat and death.

While the Philistines continue their preparations to attack Israel, some of their leaders wonder if the presence of David in their midst could be dangerous. They ask themselves if he may turn against them in the middle of the battle against Israel, which is after all his own people. David is forced to return to the land of the Philistines without taking part in the war (29:1-11). At least David and Saul will not fight each other! The Philistines with all their power attack and "the men of Israel fled from the Philistines and were slaughtered on Mount Gilboa" (31:1). Israel's defeat, predicted by Samuel, comes to pass. Now that the army has fled or is slaughtered, "the Philistines pressed Saul and his sons hard and killed Jonathan, Abinadab and Malchishua, the sons of Saul" (v. 2). Saul has lost his army and now loses his sons; the story then concentrates on the king himself. He is left alone; there is no more hope for him. "The fighting grew heavy about Saul; the bowmen took him off his guard, so that he fell wounded by the bowmen" (v. 3). It is difficult to imagine what went through Saul's mind at this moment.

Then the king, who must have given so many orders to his servants in the past, gives the last command of his life to his armour-bearer, apparently the last person still besides him, and whose function was once held by David. Saul must have been thinking of this friend and son-in-law who turned into an enemy. The king says to this soldier: "Draw your sword and run me through with it," and gives the reason why: "I do not want these uncircumcised men to come and gloat over me" (v. 4). In saying this, Saul shows some fear or dignity. He does not want to give his enemies the joy of killing, humiliating or torturing him. "But his armour-bearer was afraid and would not do it." David twice had the chance to kill Saul, but each time he had refused to do so because one does not kill the anointed of the LORD. This may also have been the reason for this armour-bearer refusing to the follow the king's order, or maybe he was just too scared. But whatever his reason, the last order of Saul the king is not executed. "So Saul took his own sword and fell on it" (v. 4).

Samson had also refused to be humiliated by the Philistines and had committed suicide in the hope of killing as many of them as possible (Judges 16:23–31). Saul's action is very different. He has no intention of killing others; he prefers self-killing to save his own dignity. And now, after own death, Saul gets some sympathy through the solidarity of the armour-bearer, who "seeing that Saul was dead, fell on his sword too and died with him" (v. 6). Samuel's prediction was right when he told Saul: "Tomorrow you and your sons will be with me" (28:19).

Saul avoided being killed and dishonoured by the Philistines, but he does not escape humiliation after his death. The next day, the Philistines find the bodies lying on

Mount Gilboa. "They cut his head and, stripping him of his armour, had it carried round the land of the Philistines to proclaim the good news to their idols and their people. They placed his armour in the temple of Astarte; they fastened his body to the wall of Beth-shan" (vv. 9-10). Not even Saul's dead body is respected.

There are, however, still a few people who risk their life to honour their king in his death and to make sure he gets an honourable funeral beside his sons. They are the people of Jabesh-gilead, who remembered what Saul did for them when they were going to be abused by the Ammonites (11:1-11). Now they want to show their gratitude to their former saviour. "They took their bones and buried them under the tamarisk of Jabesh, and fasted for seven days" (v. 13). At least Saul's dead body does not remain the hands of the uncircumcised. These fine, faithful people assure a respectful end to Saul, whose life and death are tragic.

This is the sad ending to a sad life. Or is it the end? A story describes how David is told of Saul's death (2 Samuel 1:1-16). And that story is very different from the one we just read. A young Amalekite soldier tells David that Saul on Mount Gilboa had asked him to kill him and that he thus had killed Saul. This report is totally different from the facts. This soldier is probably convinced that David will be happy about his opponent's death, and that the soldier would get good compensation for his courageous act. Sad story again! The truth of how Saul died is not respected, all so the soldier can benefit. Even in death, Saul is abused. The gain the soldier hopes for is his own death.

David then gives his elegy over Saul and Jonathan (vv. 17-27). What he says is very moving, and we hope that his words of praise and respect not only for Jonathan his friend but also for Saul are sincere. However, if David had agreed to Saul's request in their last encounter, things would have turned out differently. Saul had admitted he was wrong; he had begged David to come back and had promised not to harm him (26:21). David had refused; he had gone his own way and joined the Philistines. If he had chosen to fight the Philistines on the side of Saul, this disaster on Mount Gilboa might have been avoided. But now it is too late!

Theological Conclusion

Most readers have not given Saul a very good evaluation. They qualify his personality and his life with sayings like "From tragic hero to villain," "Tragedy of Saul," "Tragedy of fate, tragedy of flaw?" "Failure of Saul," "The rise of the lowly, the fall of the mighty," "Sinner and victim." He is even said to be a "Freudian character." A careful reading of the Saul story may inspire different feelings towards Saul: admiration, sorrow, pity, anger, condemnation and many others. But we may also conclude that Saul's life after all is very similar to the lives of many leaders.

The beginning of the story presents a fine human being. Saul has not only the physical attributes of a leader but also the character and the interior values for such position. He has a fine relationship with his father, and that is mutual. He also knows how to treat his servants with dignity; he is a gentleman who refuses to use and abuse people. He is humble and wonders if he is worthy to become king. He is above all a religious person who gives God first place in his life. Saul knows that nothing can succeed without God. He thus consults the LORD before any important decision, he proclaims a fast, he makes an oath to God, he builds an altar, he offers sacrifices – he is even willing to sacrifice his own son – and he introduces religious reform by expelling the necromancers. Together with his wife he builds a fine family and is capable of deep friendships, with Samuel and with David, for instance. One could say that he was a loving person and a person who was loved.

It is not surprising that he becomes the first king of Israel: he is well accepted for who and what he is. He becomes leader at a very difficult period in the history of Israel. Israel's political structure at the time of the judges, when each tribe remained independent, offered no chance for its survival. Israel needed a central government, a federal leader such as a king. Saul succeeds in creating some unity between the different tribes, all of whom agree to go to war with him. This political structural change obviously does not please everybody. The new structure has its advantages, but also its disadvantages. Some people object to the choice of the person of Saul, but he tolerates their criticism; he even saves these troublemakers from the hands of people who wanted to kill all opponents. Saul's internal politics were thus a success. But a king is also responsible for external affairs. He must look after the well-being of his people and above all save them from enemies. He takes this role seriously, delivering Israel from some of its enemies, such as the Ammonites and the Amalekites. He even obtains some partial victories over the Philistines. Saul cannot be held accountable for not being able to eliminate completely the Philistine danger. They had been for a long time and would still be for a while "the" enemy, nearly invincible. Everything in the beginning of Saul's career was thus extremely positive.

Whatever reading we make of the life and personality of Saul, we must take seriously how the Bible itself describes and summarizes the first part of Saul's life (14:47-52). Everything in this passage is positive. There is not one single hint of something wrong with Israel's first king. He was a family man, an administrator and an effective military commander.

But then, as we have seen, things began to go wrong. Saul is accused of disobeying God twice, and paves the way for his own downfall. The first occasion, when Samuel did not arrive when he was supposed to, was not Saul's fault, but it results in Saul losing his kingship (13:8-15). It is remarkable that Saul does not confess that he was wrong, as he did on other occasions. What happens next seems to support Saul's innocence, since his success continues. He is victorious over the Philistines and receives a positive summary of his career. The second occasion, however, is a different story. This time, in the war against the Amalekites, he does not observe one of the rules of the holy war: he and his army spare the king and the best of the animals. Now Samuel has a valid case. Even though Saul says he was saving the animals to sacrifice to the LORD, Samuel tells him he will lose his kingdom. Saul admits he was wrong, saying, "I have sinned," but begs Samuel, "forgive my sin; come back with me" (15:24-25). Samuel refuses. There is no forgiveness. Instead of coming back, Samuel breaks his friendship with Saul and they never see each other again.

After first being unjustly accused of wrong and then being refused pardon and restoration of an actual wrong, Saul changes profoundly. The text puts it very clearly: "The spirit of the LORD had left Saul and an evil spirit from the LORD filled him" (16:14). Saul's strength becomes terror, his courage becomes fear, his enthusiasm becomes depression.

Fear dominates him: fear of what will happen to him, fear of losing his kingship. To lose it, even though he never sought it, would be humiliating. He would be seen as a failure. So Saul clings to his power and prestige. Realizing that David could be the one who will take over his kingship, his fear leads to jealousy and self-pity, his jealousy fills him with anger, and his anger ends up as hatred. When a powerful leader has reached that level, he becomes dangerous. And that indeed is what Saul becomes. He accuses people who show an interest in David of conspiracy, and blames the priests, the officers, his own children and above all David himself for what is happening.

Like other leaders who see conspiracy everywhere, he moves to force. When his officers will not carry out his order to kill the priests, he commits murder himself. He tries twice to have David killed as well, but fails. Ironically, David has two opportunities to kill Saul, but instead saves the king. David's generosity changes Saul: while he can still be cruel, he admits his fault openly and does not try to justify his actions. David is not willing to reunite with Saul. Saul speaks a second time, admitting that "I have sinned" and begging David to "come back," the same things he had said to Samuel. But, like Samuel, David refuses.

Saul has gone through deep changes in his character: once as a result of Samuel's actions, and once as a result of David's. They have abandoned him, and when God does not answer him, he turns to illegal means of help from the necromancer of En-dor. In the end, the whole world seems to collapse around Saul. His circle of friends becomes smaller and smaller, until he is completely alone. The only way out that he considers honourable is suicide.

One can call Saul a failed king, but what would have been Saul's story if Samuel and David had given him their support when he asked for it? Yet the Saul story raises even more profound theological questions. Samuel is the prophet of the LORD, and proclaims the word of God, so who is that God of the Saul story? He is a God who elects and then rejects, a God who punishes apparently for no conscious fault, or whose punishment is disproportionate to the sin, and who refuses to forgive even the penitent sinner. Saul is not blameless, but he is a victim, too. His life seems to be predetermined by God − or is it by fate? The Saul story begins by illustrating the bright side of God, but then illustrates very strongly the obscure, incomprehensible dark side of God. That side of God is also presented in the Book of Job, where God sends his worst tragedies to a man who is trying to live the most exemplary life. In the story of Saul, God shows his dark side but at the same time in the same events he shows his bright side to David. In this respect the Saul story is similar to the story of Cain and Abel, where the question of why Abel and his offering were accepted and why Cain and his offering were not remains unanswered (Genesis 4:1-16).

It is always risky and difficult to use the Bible for our own questions. It seems, however, that the Saul story illustrates and confirms perhaps some of the wisdom that humanity has acquired over the centuries, and still must discover today. First, it shows the importance of the separation between Church and State. Prophets can play an important role in guiding the search for values. Samuel is of great help in clarifying that Israel could have an earthly king and that this was not an attempt to reject the kingship of the LORD. But it does not seem to be the role of a prophet to determine the person who should play that role. When Samuel anoints David while Saul is still the official king, things are doomed to go wrong. A second point that the Saul story shows is the value of democracy. Leaders or chiefs who appoint themselves or are sure to be appointed for life constitute a great danger. They may do very well in the beginning of their mandate, but when they start clinging to their position and see conspiracy everywhere, the effect on the people they are supposed to serve is disastrous. They then isolate themselves more and more until they see no way out. In our day, such failed leaders are taken out of their besieged capital by helicopter, or they commit suicide. History continues to repeat itself. The Saul story is only one example of this, but it is a precious one.

4

JONAH: A Failed Prophet
(Jonah 1–4)

Critical Observations

Jonah is probably the best-known prophet in the collection of the twelve Minor Prophets. Even people who do not read the Bible often, and who have never heard of prophets such as Obadiah, Nahum or Haggai, just to name a few others of that collection, know about Jonah. After all, it is not common for a fish to swallow a person and then vomit him onto the shore, and most people would probably not compose a psalm while sitting in the belly of a fish!

Many biblical books raise all kinds of critical questions; this little Book of Jonah, which has only four chapters, is certainly no exception. To begin with, there are a few questions concerning the book as literature. The Book of Jonah is classified as one of the prophetic books, probably because it seems to present Jonah as a prophet. But a quick comparison between this book and all the other prophetic books, both the Major and the Minor Prophets, reveals a significant difference. Normally, prophetic books contain the oracles of the prophets under whose name they are known. We read the words they proclaimed to the people of Israel in the name of the LORD. These prophetic books contain few narrative texts; it is therefore very difficult to discover much about the personal life of these prophets. Only a few texts may speak of their call or describe some important biographical events. This is not the case for the

Book of Jonah. Its content is not a collection of Jonah's oracles, but the whole book (except the psalm) presents a series of events that happened to him. The book is a narrative. All the other prophetic books, because they contain mostly oracles, are generally written in poetic form, while the Book of Jonah, since it is a narrative, is in prose. Any reader, just by opening the book, can notice this difference. The Book of Jonah, in that respect, could better be compared with the stories of the prophets Elijah and Elisha. These two prophets, however, do not have their own books; their stories are included in what we call the Historical Books (see 1 Kings 17 – 2 Kings 13). One wonders, therefore, how the Book of Jonah ended up where it did in our canon.

Still taking the book in itself as literature, we notice that three of the four chapters are prose (1:1–2:2, 11; 3–4) while in between these narratives a poem suddenly appears. This poem is the psalm Jonah composed while he was in the belly of the fish (2:3-10). Biblical scholars using diachronic approaches agree, for all kind of reasons, that this psalm does not fit well into the book; they therefore consider the psalm a later insertion. This will become rather clear in the reading of the text. At this point, it may suffice to look at just one verse of the psalm. Jonah prays: "I remembered the LORD, and my prayer came before you into your holy Temple" (2:8). The belly of a fish is not exactly the Temple! But in a synchronic reading, we can see why this prayer was placed here.

The Book of Jonah also raises serious historical questions. The book opens with the statement that the word of the LORD was addressed to "Jonah son of Amittai" (1:1). At the time when Jeroboam II was king in Israel, there was a prophet called "Jonah son of Amittai" who was identified as the "prophet from Gath-hepher" (2 Kings 14:25). This suggests that this Jonah of the book lived in the eighth century BCE. But the Book of Jonah does not address issues of that period at all, and contains no reference to king Jeroboam II. Besides that, the prophet Jonah does not preach to his own people, as prophets generally do; he proclaims God's word only to the people of Nineveh. The more we read the Book of Jonah, the more it becomes evident that this book is not history. There are no historical references, as we find in other prophetic books. Such references are often found in the book's title (compare, for instance, Amos 1:1). Many details that we would expect to find in a historical book are missing. Here are a few examples. The name of the land where the fish vomited Jonah on the shore is not given (2:11). The text speaks of "the king of Nineveh" (3:6) without revealing his name, contrary to what is done in other prophetic books. And above all, most readers may be surprised to learn, the book is a sequence of miracles. There is nothing wrong with that in itself, but the number of them and the kind of marvellous or strange things that happen in just a few chapters is certainly suspicious. They happen from beginning till end: the unexpected storm at sea, the sailors finding the guilty one by casting lots, the story of the fish, the amazing things that happen with the plant that grows and withers in no time. The more we read, the more we wonder about the historicity of this little book.

A good writer must help the reader to find out the literary genre of his writing, or else miss his purpose. The writer of the Book of Jonah does this in a few small details. He writes: "Now Nineveh was a city great beyond compare: it took three days to cross it" (3:3). But it does not take three days to cross big modern cities, and if we look at the dimensions of most old cities in the Ancient Near East, it obviously would not take three days to pass through Nineveh. Note that Jonah has also spent three days in the belly of the fish (2:1). The number three in the Bible is often a symbolic number that expresses fullness. Jonah preaches to the people of Nineveh and tells them that the city has only "forty days more" before it will be totally destroyed. The number forty reminds us of the flood (Genesis 7:4) and of the period Israel spent in the desert (Numbers 14:34). This number corresponds to a period of purification and punishment – see also the forty days in the life of Elijah (1 Kings 19:8). The writer describes Nineveh as "the great city, in which there are more than a hundred and twenty thousand people" (4:11). That number indicates universalism (Judith 2:5, 15). The numbers the writer uses seem mostly symbolic. That the text is not historical is also confirmed by the fact that none of the numerous extra-biblical Assyrian texts that are at our disposal mentions the conversion of Nineveh. For all these reasons, it is obvious that the Book of Jonah is not a book of history or geography. The writer uses the name of a prophet found in the Book of Kings of whom we know basically nothing to write a text that belongs to the category of fiction. It is a marvellous story full of images comparable to prophetic legends.

The Bible contains many texts that are fictional. Jesus himself loved to speak in parables. Such stories have two purposes; to entertain and to instruct. That the Book of Jonah entertains is evident: everyone knows and enjoys that story. One can call it humour, irony or satire, but it is certainly entertaining. The book also tries to instruct. The writer reacts against the narrow-mindedness of many people in Israel after the time of the exile (400–200 BCE). The people needed to hear that the LORD does not care only about Israel, but even cares about their enemies.

I have chosen Jonah to illustrate another biblical human failure. It is often said that most prophets failed, in the sense that their message rarely received the acceptance they were hoping for. This generalization has to be qualified, since all prophets had their own support group, and their preaching is still read now after all these centuries. So prophets had at least some success; but still, they often had to cope with resistance. Except for Jonah. His mission succeeded perfectly; the people of Nineveh fully accepted his invitation to conversion. But what a failure Jonah is as a person! He is a sad and failed prophet.

The Story of Jonah

One day Jonah experienced a unique and intimate encounter with God: "The word of the LORD was addressed to Jonah son of Amittai" (1:1). Many prophets and other people discover in such moments that God calls them for a special function and mission. The person suddenly realizes what orientation his or her life should take. That is exactly what happened to Jonah that day of his life. The name "Jonah" means "dove." The Bible does not often speak of doves, but a few texts are significant. The prophet Hosea compares Israel to "a silly, witless dove calling on Egypt, turning to Assyria" (Hosea 7:11). Jonah, as we shall see, also appears to be a silly dove, not going to Nineveh but to Tarshish. Noah sends out a dove from his ark to find out if the flood is over (Genesis 8:6-12). The dove's failure to return announces good news to Noah. The LORD also wants to send a dove to Nineveh, but the dove does not want to go at first.

These were the words Jonah received on that special day: "Up, go to Nineveh, the great city, and inform them that their wickedness has become known to me" (v. 2). God asks Jonah to get up, which suggests that he has to leave his too-easy life and get involved. That involvement, his mission, is to go to Nineveh. That is not exactly like going to the next street, to the next village or town. According to the story, Jonah son of Amittai came from "Gath-hepher" (2 Kings 24:25), a small place 20 kilometres west of Tiberias. He had probably not seen much of the world, but if he had, none of what he may have seen could compare to Nineveh, frequently called "the great city" in the book of Jonah. It may have sounded exciting to go and see that magnificent place of whose splendour he may have heard, but it must also have been frightening for him. To go to Nineveh was a long trip – over a thousand kilometres – and above all, these Assyrians were not exactly the best friends of the people in Israel. All other prophets before Jonah had been sent to their own people; only Amos, who came from the southern kingdom, was sent elsewhere – to the northern kingdom, which after all was still very close. But he was not well received and was quickly expelled (Amos 7:11-13). Who wants to be criticized? Even worse, who wants to be criticized and judged by a foreigner? And the message that Jonah has to give the people of Nineveh is a harsh criticism; he has to blame them for their great wickedness. Jonah knows that the Ninevites will not want to hear that. On the other hand, he may have felt very happy knowing that God punishes sinners. So if the wickedness of Nineveh were that great, the divine punishment would be proportionately great. Jonah may have felt that finally the Assyrians would pay for all their crimes, especially for those committed against his own people. Nineveh was the capital of Assyria, which had destroyed the kingdom of Israel.

Jonah does not say one word in response to the LORD's call; he simply decides what he wants to do and acts upon it: "Jonah decided to run away from the LORD, and to go to Tarshish." He loses no time in following up on his decision:"He went down to Joppa and found a ship bound for Tarshish; he paid his fare and went aboard, to go with them to Tarshish, to get away from the LORD" (v. 3). This is a first in the history of Israel: not only is Jonah the first prophet to be sent to such a faraway country, he is also the first prophet to put aside God's call. Other prophets resisted their call, but they entered into dialogue with God and gave him in all honesty their reasons for resisting. Moses told God that he was not a good speaker (Exodus 4:10-13);

Jeremiah objected that his words would have no impact since he was too young (Jeremiah 1:6-8). Jonah does not say one word. Why, then, did he refuse his mission? It was certainly not the long trip to a foreign land that frightened him, since he decides to go to Tarshish, which is also far away. Tarshish is often presented in the Bible as being the end of the world (Psalm 48:7; 72:10). Its precise location is uncertain – probably in Spain, but it could also be in Sardinia, or in Tunisia. So instead of going to the far east, Jonah goes to the far west! He even dares to take a ship, which was rare for people of Israel at that time. It is thus not the trip to Nineveh that must have caused Jonah's refusal; we can therefore only guess that he was too afraid to preach that severe accusation to the Assyrians. He had valid reasons to expect them to react violently, for that was how even the people of Israel at times treated their prophets. If this is the right answer, we are still left with a mystery. Jonah could have refused and stayed home. Why does he decide to leave home and to travel to Tarshish (repeated three times), exactly in the opposite direction from Nineveh? To that question the text seems to provide an answer. Jonah must have realized that God was not pleased with his refusal, and he may have feared God's punishment for his disobedience. He therefore tries to escape as far as possible "away from the LORD" (twice). People at that time believed that God was only present in the land inhabited by his believers.

The LORD, however, has other ways to find the escaping prophet. He unleashes a terrible wind that provokes a big storm. The ship Jonah is sailing on is in danger of breaking up. The sailors, who are the experts of the sea, know that this storm is serious; they "took fright." They must have been from different countries, since each one starts praying to his own god. They do more than just pray: they know by experience that if they throw some of the cargo overboard, the ship may be easier to pilot. Jonah, who apparently refused to go to Nineveh out of fear of preaching that severe message, and who now tries to escape from God out of fear of God's possible punishment for his disobedience, is the only one who does not seem to be frightened: "Jonah had fallen asleep" (v. 5). After all the emotions he experienced after being called by God for an impossible mission, Jonah is convinced that he is safe now. He is moving farther and farther away from God, and he has paid for his trip, so he can relax and sleep. He is not going to lose any more sleep over his refusal of the divine call. Notice that the "pagan" sailors are praying, but the prophet of the Lord is sleeping!

Now the sailors take over and wonder about their passenger. Like the Lord had said to Jonah: "Up! … inform the people of Nineveh," the sailors say to Jonah: "Get up! Call on your God" (v. 6). Since each one of them had prayed to his own god but nothing had happened, Jonah should pray to his God, too. The text does not say whether Jonah prayed or not. He may not have been too keen to call on the Lord, from whom he is trying to escape! Since the sailors' prayers did not help, they wonder if someone on the ship is guilty of some hidden crime. They decide to draw lots and "the lot fell on Jonah" (v. 7). They are thus convinced that this terrible storm is his fault. Jonah is obliged to identify himself: "I am a Hebrew, and I worship the Lord, the God of heaven, who made the sea and the land" (v. 9). The sailors, who have already taken fright because of the storm, "were seized with terror" after hearing this answer. They have good reason to be afraid. If the Lord, the God of Jonah, is master of land and sea, as Jonah claims, then that God is causing this terrible storm. This must have something to do with Jonah. The sailors thus raise a very valid question: "What have you done?" (v. 10). Jonah has no choice but to tell them that he is trying to escape from the Lord his God. But one wonders about what Jonah says, believes and does. If Jonah really believes

what he says to the sailors, that the LORD is indeed the God
who made the sea and the land, how could he hope to
get away from the LORD by going to Tarshish? The LORD's
power is thus not limited to the land of Israel: the LORD
is master of the sea and of the far ends of the world, and
thus also of Tarshish, where Jonah wants to go.

What to do now? Because of the storm, the sailors
cannot continue their trip to Tarshish, nor can they bring
Jonah back to Joppa. And the storm does not give any sign
of letting up: on the contrary, "the sea was growing rougher
and rougher" (v. 11). Since Jonah has caused the trouble,
they ask him what solution he suggests. Jonah answers:
"Take me and throw me into the sea, and then it will grow
calm for you. For I can see it is my fault this violent storm
has happened to you" (v. 12). Here Jonah shows that he is a
courageous person, ready to sacrifice himself for others. He
knows that the lives of all are in his hands; his death may
save all the sailors. He may be regretting that he refused
the divine call! These sailors seem to be very fine people.
They hesitate to send Jonah to his certain death. They start
rowing even harder, but no hope is in sight; "the sea grew
still rougher for them" (v. 13).

The sailors have no remaining options. Jonah must be
right. After exhausting all their human efforts, they turn
to God once more in prayer. But this time they address
themselves to the LORD, the God of Jonah. "O LORD, do
not let us perish for taking this man's life; do not hold us
guilty of innocent blood; for you, LORD, have acted as you
have thought right" (v. 14). They still are afraid to offend
God by sacrificing Jonah. They pray that this action will not
make them offend the LORD, whom Jonah has disobeyed.
After their prayer, "taking hold of Jonah they threw him
into the sea." The miracle happens: the rough sea "grew
calm again" in one instant (v. 15). This proves clearly that
the storm was a punishment for Jonah's escape from the

Lord, and that the Lord does not blame the sailors for throwing Jonah overboard.

These sailors are fine religious people; in their joy that the danger is over, they do not forget to thank the Lord. "At this the men were seized with dread of the Lord; they offered a sacrifice to the Lord and made vows" (v. 16). Jonah had refused his prophetic mission for Nineveh; yet in running away from that mission he has unwillingly become a witness of the Lord to these sailors and caused them to recognize the Lord's power, which perhaps points to their conversion. It appears that, at least in his death, Jonah has accomplished something. Strange way of being a prophet! This appears to be the end of the story of the prophet Jonah.

To Jonah's surprise, and the reader's, it is not the end. (I hope that the sailors, too, learned the rest of the story.) The Lord has indeed heard the sailors' prayers; they are not guilty of taking the prophet's life. For Jonah does not drown in the sea. God has other plans: "the Lord had arranged that a great fish should be there to swallow Jonah" (2:1a). The text does not say what kind of fish it is. It may have been a whale, a walrus or a sea cow – not a shark, we hope. It must have been a big fish if it could swallow a man. What a frightening experience for Jonah! Disappearing into the waves of the sea was bad enough, but seeing a big fish coming towards you ready to swallow you up would be even worse. Even more curious is that "Jonah remained in the belly of the fish for three days and three nights" (v. 1b). How he ever survived there for three days is of course a new mystery. He must still be in good health, since he finds the strength to do something inside that fish. We do not know if Jonah prayed to the Lord on the ship, but now "from the belly of the fish he prayed to the Lord, his God" (v. 2). Nobody has to force Jonah this time. He prays on his own.

We as readers are fortunate to have the text of Jonah's prayer recorded in the fish's belly. Jonah begins with: "Out of my distress I cried to the LORD and he answered me; from the belly of Sheol I cried, and you have heard my voice" (v. 3). The prayer follows the structure of the psalms of thanksgiving. The person begins with a description of his sufferings and miseries and then continues by explaining how he was saved from them. It has not been easy so far to follow how Jonah thinks and acts, but it becomes even more and more difficult. He thanks God for having saved him, but how can Jonah say that he is saved? He may be saved from drowning, but now he is in the belly of a fish. I wonder if he is in a better position. How can a human person survive in the belly of a fish, with no food, no water and, after three days, not much air? Jonah, inside the fish, is doomed to die, probably a slower and more painful death than drowning. And even if he were to survive inside that fish, what kind of life would that be?

But we go from one surprise to another in this little book. The LORD does not want Jonah to die; he wants him alive. That the fish was in that spot when the sailors threw Jonah into the sea was not pure coincidence; as the text says, "the LORD had arranged" it (v. 1). God has a plan. And so "the LORD spoke to the fish" with Jonah in his belly. We don't know what God told the fish, but we may surmise from what the fish does what God must have ordered. The fish "vomited Jonah on the shore" (v. 11). Jonah is alive! The LORD has saved him; he has heard Jonah's prayer. Jonah was right to thank the LORD. His prayer may have expressed his deep confidence that God would somehow come to his rescue. It was a prayer of thanksgiving in advance. But on what shore did the fish vomit Jonah? The text of the Book of Jonah leaves a lot of questions unanswered. Did the fish bring Jonah back to Joppa, where he had taken the boat to run away from the LORD? That would likely not have taken three days. So did the fish bring Jonah through seas and rivers to the river Tigris, close to the city of Nineveh? That would have been quite a voyage, but that is where the LORD wanted Jonah to go. Maybe God helped the obstinate prophet a little bit.

Since the LORD saved Jonah from certain death, he obviously has a plan for him. Jonah does not have to wait long to find out what that plan is. "The word of the LORD was addressed a second time to Jonah" (3:1). In Jonah's second encounter with God, the LORD repeats in the exact same words what he said before: "Up! Go to Nineveh, the great city." This time he adds "and denounce it in the words I will give you" (v. 2). The first time, the LORD said: "inform them that their wickedness has become known to me" (1:2). This time he indicates that he will tell Jonah what to say to the people in Nineveh after he gets there. God does not take any chances with Jonah this time.

Of course we wonder how Jonah is going to react. That is what he does: "Jonah set out and went to Nineveh in obedience to the word of the LORD" (v. 3a). The first time, Jonah refused his mission; this time he accepts and, as the text specifies, in full obedience to God. This is rather surprising. The first time, we guessed that he was afraid to accuse Nineveh. He was sure that this message would be an unwelcome one, and that the Ninevites could throw him out, imprison him, or even kill him. This time, Jonah does not know exactly what he is to tell the people in Nineveh; he only knows that it will be an accusation since he has to "denounce" them. He still has reason to be afraid. But he has paid dearly for not accepting God's call the first time. Poor Jonah does not have much choice; he decides that he would rather take his chances in Nineveh. It cannot be worse than what he has just gone through.

Jonah finally arrives in that great city that he had never seen before. Coming from the insignificant country of Israel, he must have felt lost. He realizes that it will take him "three days" to cross it (v. 3). Spending three days in the city of his enemies may seem to him as bad as spending three days in the belly of the fish. From his first day of walking in Nineveh, Jonah proclaims, "Only forty days more and Nineveh is going to be destroyed" (v. 4). When God called him the second time, he did not reveal yet what Jonah was supposed to proclaim to the people of Nineveh. But even though the text does not say it explicitly, we may suppose that after Jonah entered the city God told him what to preach. This message is different from the first one. The first time, he was to accuse the people of their great wickedness; this time, he proclaims the total destruction of that great city. We may conclude that this destruction is the divine punishment for their wickedness. But somehow, this announcement is even worse. If Jonah was afraid that the people of Nineveh would react violently to his accusation, how must he feel now? There is, however, an important and perhaps reassuring detail. The destruction will not happen today, but in "forty days." It is not that long a period – only forty days – but still many things could happen during this time.

And indeed, strange things do happen. We face another surprise in the text. These Ninevites, far from getting angry with Jonah, expelling him or treating him violently, do something unexpected. "And the people of Nineveh believed in God; they proclaimed a fast and put on sackcloth, from the greatest to the least" (v. 5). They make the rituals of penance as a sign of their conversion. The people in Israel rarely reacted this way to the preaching of the prophets. Jonah's task was not that difficult after all. The people respond to him; they accept his preaching.

Besides fearing the people, Jonah may have had a special fear of the authorities, especially the king of Nineveh. Its kings could be very cruel towards their enemies. Even the kings of Israel were not always open to the preaching of the prophets, as in the case of Jeremiah (Jeremiah 36). But the king of Nineveh has a different reaction: "The news reached the king of Nineveh, who rose from his throne, took off his robe, put on sackcloth and sat down in ashes" (v. 6). Prophets have often predicted that those who elevate themselves will be humbled; this king humbles himself. He even puts all his authority behind an order he gives to his people: "A proclamation was then promulgated throughout Nineveh, by decree of the king and his ministers." It looks as if Jonah does not even have to continue going through the streets of Nineveh; his work is done for him by royal decree. The king decides that "Men and beasts, herds and flocks, are to taste nothing; they must not eat. They must not drink water" (v. 7). He does not say for how long they have to fast, but Jonah may be reminded of his fast in the belly of the fish. The royal decree continues: "All are to put on sackcloth and call on God with all their might."

Besides all these rituals, the king requires of all the people something even more important and fundamental: "and let everyone renounce his evil behaviour and the wicked things he has done" (v. 8). In the first call, the LORD had charged Jonah with informing the people of Nineveh about their wickedness; the second time, the LORD had told Jonah to "denounce" them. The king and the people know they have been wicked and are willing to renounce that. The king concludes: "Who knows if God will not change his mind and relent, if he will not renounce his burning wrath, so that we do not perish?" (v. 9) Jonah has preached that the city will be destroyed. The king realizes that this is a punishment for the Ninevites' evil behaviour (including his own). If they all "renounce" their wickedness, then God may also "renounce" his wrath. Jonah has proclaimed only an accusation and the punishment; the king speaks about conversion and grace. But he realizes that even with conversion, Nineveh has no right to expect that grace; grace always remains a free gift of God.

The LORD accepts their goodwill and "he did not inflict on them the disaster which he had threatened"

(v. 10). This is a unique success story of the Bible. How often did that happen, even for Israel? How many prophets could glorify over such a success of their preaching? Great prophets such as Elijah and Jeremiah got so discouraged about the resistance they met from the people, the king or other authorities that they were tempted to give up their prophetic mission. Jonah could not have hoped for a more positive response, and it is nearly instantaneous. Only after one day of preaching, the great city of Nineveh converts. He must have felt relieved; instead of resistance and violence, he encounters acceptance. He may have been thinking how he could have saved himself a lot of trouble and misery if he had accepted his call the first time. He never would have had the trauma of the storm, the sea and the fish. He realizes now that there was really no reason to refuse God's call. This would be a good time for him to pray his psalm of thanksgiving, but he does not.

The Book of Jonah has another surprise in store for us. Instead of being pleased with what has happened, "Jonah was very indignant at this; he fell into a rage" (4:1). This seems incomprehensible. What other prophet would have reacted this way? The text has spoken of God's "burning wrath" because of the great wickedness of Nineveh; now Jonah, a prophet – a person who feels and thinks as God does – falls into a "rage" because these same people renounce their evil conduct and convert. Why is Jonah so angry?

Jonah explains it in his prayer to God. This is not a prayer of thanksgiving, as we might expect after his successful mission in Nineveh. Unlike his prayer in the belly of the fish, where he thanks God for his own salvation, here he begins with a complaint or a lamentation. "Ah! LORD, is not this just as I said would happen when I was still at home? That was why I went and fled to Tarshish: I knew that you were a God of tenderness and compassion, slow to anger, rich in graciousness, relenting from evil" (v. 2).

This is the biggest surprise of the book. Jonah admits that he had foreseen what would happen if he accepted his mission to go and accuse the people of Nineveh of their great wickedness (see 1:2). He knew that God would not execute what he was supposed to preach: 'that Nineveh was going to be destroyed" (3:4). He thus had "feared" that these people would convert and that God, exactly as he did, would "relent" (3:10). Jonah had foreseen all that because he knows the real nature of the LORD, as God had revealed it to Moses (Exodus 34:6-7; see also Psalm 103:8-10). The LORD's compassion is greater than his anger; he is a relenting God. In this reply, Jonah gives an unexpected answer to the question that we as readers have been asking ourselves: Why did Jonah refuse his mission without even stating his objection? We now realize that we had guessed wrong. He did not refuse because he was afraid that the Ninevites would harm him, a foreigner. He refused because he was sure that his mission would succeed, that the people of Nineveh would convert and that God would relent. That may explain why he did not formulate his objection to God, as some other prophets did when they were called. What a strange prophet, this Jonah!

Jonah continues his prayer, adding a petition to his lamentation: "So now LORD, please take away my life, for I might as well be dead as go on living" (v. 3). A joyful event makes Jonah sad; the lives of the people of Nineveh are saved, while Jonah prefers to die!

This whole story is absurd, especially if we compare Jonah's story with that of the prophet Elijah. There are many similarities between these two, but in complete opposition. Elijah, far from being well received, knows that Queen Jezebel wants to kill him, so he goes into the wilderness. Discouraged at of the apparent failure of his mission, he prays to God: "Take my life" (1 Kings 19:1-8). Jonah, on the other hand, is well received by the king of Nineveh and is not in any danger of being killed. His mission is very successful, and yet he prays, "take my life"!

The LORD, surprised like everyone else, replies, "Are you right to be angry?" (v. 4). Jonah is not a person who likes to justify his actions. He did not explain to God why he refused the mission; he simply left for Tarshish. This time, too, instead of giving his reasons, he moves on: "Jonah then went out of the city and sat down to the east of the city. There he made himself a shelter and sat under it in the shade" (v. 5). He does what Elijah had done. Elijah, in his discouragement, went "to sit under a furze bush wishing he were dead" (1 Kings 19:4). Does Jonah also sit under his shelter waiting for the death he hopes for? In fact, this is not Jonah's intention; he sits there "to see what would happen to the city" (v. 5). But what could happen? The people of Nineveh have converted; God has relented and will not destroy the city. Is Jonah still hoping that somehow the city will be destroyed? Does he wait to see if their conversion will not be a lasting one? He may have to sit there for a long time!

If the LORD can show mercy to the people of Nineveh, he is not going to reject his strange prophet who is so full of self-pity. God had once saved Jonah by "arranging" to send that fish. This time the LORD, looking at that poor shelter, wants to protect Jonah better: "the LORD arranged that a castor-oil plant should grow up over Jonah to give shade for his head and soothe his ill-humour" (v. 6a). Indeed, Jonah, who seems to have lost all common sense, needs his head to be protected! And it works. "Jonah was delighted with the castor-oil plants" (v. 6b). Finally, a smile appears on the face of this angry prophet; he can laugh at life again for a short moment.

But, as so often happens in this story, we get another surprise – this time from God. After arranging for that castor-oil plant to give shade to Jonah, "at dawn the next day, God arranged that a worm should attack the castor-oil plant – and it withered" (v. 7). And that is not all. "Next, when the sun rose, God arranged that there should be a scorching east wind; the sun beat down so hard on Jonah's head that he was overcome" (v. 8a). Jonah has been sitting and waiting, hoping to see the destruction of Nineveh. Now he sees another kind of destruction: the plant giving him shade withers. His poor head! That he would now have strange ideas is understandable. His smile is gone and he falls back into his previous wish and prayer; this time he even begs for it: "I might as well be dead as go on living" (v. 8b).

Twice Jonah has expressed the same wish for death, and twice God gives him the same answer: "Are you right to be angry?" (v. 9) Is Jonah right to be angry that God saved Nineveh and that God gave and then took away the castor-oil plant? For the first time in his life, Jonah formulates an answer to God instead of just ignoring God's question. His answer is clear and full of anger: "I have every right to be angry, to the point of death" (v. 9). We may find that he has a point: it is strange for a plant to grow and wither like that.

God replies with a kind of accusation of Jonah that turns into a question. The LORD challenges the prophet. How is it possible that "you," Jonah, are so angry about "only a castor-oil plant" for which you have not even done anything? Why should Jonah get angry about something so insignificant that appeared in one night and disappeared in one night? Then follows the central question: "And am 'I' not to feel sorry for Nineveh, the great city?" (vv. 10-11). Here the dialogue ends, and Jonah falls back into his habit of not giving answers to God.

The LORD's question is not only the end of the conversation but also the end of the book. We still wait for Jonah's answer. The book opens with a word of God calling Jonah. It ends with God addressing a question to Jonah. Both times, the prophet does not answer. Did he ever come to accept that he was wrong? Did he ever come to a conversion the way the Ninevites did? We don't know. What a strange prophet. What a failure!

Theological Conclusion

The story of Jonah often causes people to laugh. It is indeed more enjoyable to read the Book of Jonah than the Book of Leviticus with all its laws. Jonah at least is an enjoyable story! But the story is not funny at all. It is another sad story of the Bible. The Book of Jonah is full of surprises; a few are happy surprises, but most are sad ones.

Its main actor is a narrow-minded, closed, angry person who is full of self-pity. He is a man who has no joy in his life and who does not want other people to find joy and happiness. As a human being Jonah is a disaster, and that he is a prophet makes it even worse. All the other characters in the story deserve respect and admiration. The sailors are deeply religious people afraid to offend their god and their neighbour; they only reluctantly come to accept Jonah's proposal to throw him into the sea. The people of Nineveh were certainly no saints, but they are open to God's word and ready to change their lives.

A prophet, by definition, is a man of God, a person who lives in close union with God, who thinks and feels as God does, who rejoices with God and suffers with God. Jonah has none of these qualities. When God calls him, he is not interested in the least. He is, of course, not the only person who has difficulty accepting God's call; that is perfectly human. But a decent person would at least explain why. He would enter into dialogue with God, so that God can reassure him or help him to see the purpose of it all. Not Jonah. He does not give reasons for his refusal, which may be just as well, because they are selfish, horrible reasons. God wants Jonah to help people become conscious of their wickedness, to convert and so to become good people. But Jonah does not want to do this because these people are not his people; they are foreigners and even enemies. He wants their total destruction and not their salvation. He would rather they die than live.

His life is not only a categorical refusal of God's call; he even tries to get as far away from God as he can. Spiritually, he is not attuned to God; he also wants to separate himself from God physically. But nobody can escape God, since God is creator and master of the universe. Jonah knows and believes that, but he still tries to hide. There is no harmony between his beliefs and his actions.

But despite all his stubbornness, he cannot escape God and unwillingly has to submit to him. When Jonah has no other choice but to accept his mission, he does so mechanically, without enthusiasm. His heart is not in it. Any other normal person, and certainly a prophet, would rejoice in the success of his mission, to see people accept God's word and change their lives. Yet Jonah instead of rejoicing becomes very angry. He even keeps a hidden hope that this conversion will not be real and that God will still punish these Ninevites.

The life of every human person is often a mixture of good and bad. Jonah has some goodness in him, too. Rather than causing the deaths of several people at sea, he admits that he is to blame for the storm. He is even ready to sacrifice his own life so that the sailors may be saved. He knows that God is in command, even if he does not always act according to his beliefs. At least once in his life Jonah thanks God, grateful that God has saved his life. He even does this before he is saved; he thanks God in advance, convinced that he will be saved from the belly of that fish.

Jonah thus shows that he knows how to pray to God and to enter in dialogue with God, but the general attitude of his life is very different. When God initiates a dialogue with him, Jonah answers only once. That is when God asks Jonah if he has the right to be angry. He does not have to search long for his answer; he replies that without any doubt he has that right. He answers in order to confirm and justify his own attitude. But he never answers if he feels this would imply giving in to God or admitting his mistake. And so Jonah refuses to answer God when he is called at the beginning of the book, and he refuses to answer God at the end when God challenges him to a conversion of heart and to admit his error and narrow-mindedness. Jonah had shown that he could take the initiative to enter in dialogue with God when he formulated a prayer of thanksgiving. He does it again in a prayer of supplication, in which he begs to die. Jonah has said one prayer of thanksgiving for being saved, and one prayer in which he asks to die. If God had accepted that prayer, Jonah would have died in his anger. His death as well as his life would have been sad. Indeed, people often die as they live.

In the collection of human biblical failures, Jonah certainly deserves a place of honour. He is a person whose life could have been successful and happy if he had been open to God and others. He could have avoided much trouble and trials at sea and in the fish, and he could have rejoiced in the success of his mission and in the salvation of the Ninevites. Other prophets would have envied him for such an accomplishment, so rare in the life of a prophet. But since Jonah is closed to God and to others, his life is wasted in anger, and the only way out he can see is death. While Samson and Saul took their own lives, Jonah prays that God will do this for him. What a failed prophet!

5

JUDAS: *A Failed Apostle*
(The Gospels)

Critical Observations

The preceding four examples of biblical human failures – Lot, Samson, Saul and Jonah – are all taken from the Old Testament, but failure is also present in the New Testament. Success and failure are indeed part of human existence at all times and places. The best-known human failure in the New Testament is without doubt the Judas story. Many people may laugh while reading the Jonah story, and some perhaps even while reading the Samson story. Not too many will find the Lot and Saul stories amusing. But there is absolutely nothing to laugh about concerning Judas and his life. His story is the saddest of them all, and Judas is a tragic figure.

It is more complicated to study Judas than the other four characters we have looked at. It was easy to determine the limits of their stories. Most of them covered a certain number of chapters in a specific biblical book, but for Judas there is no such unified story. The only information we have about this apostle is scattered over the four gospels and in one short text in the Acts of the Apostles. Most of the time the information is given in a few verses inside another story. But even these rare texts, like many other biblical texts, raise all kind of problems for the critical reader.

For some of the preceding characters that we have studied, we noticed that the same event may be reported twice. This happened frequently in the stories of Samson and Saul. Scholars using a diachronic approach to the Bible generally explain this by suggesting that there are different sources or layers in the story. We have seen that a synchronic reading can also make a lot of sense, and that these repetitions in the story can have a particular purpose. For the Judas story, the problem is entirely different. The same event concerning Judas is often reported in all or at least in several gospels, but at times with significant variations. Here we cannot consider these texts as simple repetitions and read them synchronically. These texts refer to the same event but are presented from different angles, viewpoints or theologies. And thus this literary question leads to historical questions. What really happened and how?

A few events in the life of Judas are mentioned in all four gospels, some are found only in one or two gospels, and in the Gospel of John are a few verses that simply hint at Judas. The study of this biblical character of the New Testament will thus proceed in a different way from that used for the Old Testament failures. Following a theory about the synoptic gospels (Matthew, Mark and Luke), I will use the Gospel of Mark as my starting point and then indicate and reflect upon differences that appear in the other gospels. Of course I will also study the events of the life of Judas that are particular to other gospels if they do not appear in Mark.

We have noticed several times that biblical texts are written by the winners, and that it would be interesting to hear the voice of the losers, too, but they have disappeared. (This is very noticeable in the Saul story, but also applies to the New Testament.) Keep this thought in mind while reading the Judas story. There is indeed something remarkable, even depressing and shocking, in any of the four gospels: each time the name of Judas appears, we find an addition: "the one who was going to betray (or who betrayed) Jesus," or Judas "the traitor," or "the betrayer."

That is how Judas is always portrayed, from the first time his name appears until the end. There is one exception: "Judas – this was not Judas Iscariot – said to him…" (John 14:22). This text refers to Judas Iscariot only in order to distinguish him from another Judas; this is the only time, in this insignificant note, that there is no reference to his betrayal. This insistence and continual repetition of "traitor" is a rather sad thing to find in the New Testament. Even before the apostle did anything wrong, the reader knows what he will do later. Obviously the winners, those who made it, wrote these texts. Not that these writers and those in whose name they wrote were all that good. Peter denied Jesus three times, even after he had promised never to do so. The apostles, except John, were nowhere to be seen when Jesus died on the cross. So the eleven of the Twelve who made it had no reason to be very proud of themselves. They had not been great heroes, either. But it is always gratifying to find someone to blame. Consequently, by insisting each time that Judas is "the traitor," they found the one to blame for Jesus' death. This must have made them feel less guilty about not showing much courage at that critical moment in Jesus' life. The repeated statement "Judas the traitor" may say more about the writers than about Judas.

We do not have the gospel according to Judas. He never wrote one, and if he had, his gospel would have disappeared and would never have made it into the canon. But such a story written by the loser would have been a precious document for us readers. We know what others say about him, but how did Judas see his own life? Why did he become the traitor? Are the reasons the ones that we find in the gospels, or are there other, hidden reasons that we only can guess at? If we read and compare the gospel texts related to the same event in the life of Judas, we notice that there has been a tendency to give him more and more blame, and to make things perhaps worse than they were.

Many readers of the Old Testament get upset about some of the things they find there, such as the killing that goes on, some of which is at the LORD's command. More and more readers today point out that biblical texts are written from the male perspective; feminist readings reveal the patriarchal character of the Bible. In a world where anti-Semitism is again on the rise, some scholars wonder if the roots of that evil lie in the gospels. Several scholars accuse especially the Gospel of John of containing texts that are offensive to Jewish people. It has becomes a custom in the Church today that the authorities ask forgiveness for what happened during the crusades or other historical events. It may be time to become conscious of these derogatory tendencies towards Judas in the biblical texts and see that they are stronger in some gospels than in others.

No single human person is perfect. Everyone does stupid things at one time or another, and I am no exception. If, from that moment on, my name is then automatically linked with such a sad event, and if each time people say, "You know, that is the one who did…," such behaviour would reveal more about the people who speak this way than about my weakness. Judas may be the traitor, but is it fair that this identifier is added to his name each time he appears in the gospels? Even worse, his very name has taken on that meaning; "he is a real Judas" is not a compliment. It may be time for us to recognize that the gospels are not terribly Christian in that respect. In any family where there is love and understanding, people would show more respect for their brother or sister. Judas, too, is a Christian; he is a brother of us Christians. We could show more respect for Judas; we could try to find out why Judas betrayed Jesus. That would probably help us show him a little more understanding. Let us not make the tragedy of his life even worse than it was.

As with the four other failed characters of the Bible studied in this book, my intention is not to search for what happened historically; and I do not wish to blame or judge Judas. We will simply read the texts and try to discover why, according to these texts, Judas became the failed apostle.

The Story of Judas

Judas appears in the gospels for the first time when Jesus appoints and chooses the Twelve: "He now went up into the hills and summoned those he wanted. So they came to him and he appointed Twelve; they were to be his companions and to be sent out to preach, with power to cast out devils. And so he appointed the Twelve: Simon to whom he gave the name Peter, James…and Judas Iscariot, the man who was to betray him" (Mark 3:13-19). A similar text concerning the election or the mission of the Twelve is found in Matthew (10:2-5) and in Luke (6:12-16).

Some differences appear between the three lists, but they all agree in what they say about Judas. First of all, in the three lists he is always mentioned at the end. Of course, someone has to be placed at the end of a list, but why is it always Judas? Was he the last to be chosen by Jesus? Does the list follow the chronological order of their call? Or was Judas placed there because the tradition really considered him the "last," the least important? That seems to be the most plausible answer, and the reason for this is easy to find: after all, he is the traitor!

Second, in all three lists he is always given the name "Judas Iscariot" (John refers to him this way, too [12:4], but he also speaks of "Judas son of Simon Iscariot" [6:71] and "Judas Iscariot, son of Simon" [13:2]). That double name makes Judas different from the others. Most of the time they are listed just by their name, at times they are said to be the son of so-and-so, but none of them has a double name. There is a discussion on the meaning of "Iscariot," but it is generally understood as "man of Kerioth," referring to the place Judas came from. Keriot was a town in Judah (Joshua 15:25). That is an interesting detail, and if all four gospels mention it, it must be an important piece of information. We know that all the other apostles came from Galilee and therefore from the North. Judas, however, came from Judah and thus from the South. We know what several other apostles did in life before Jesus called them: some were fishermen, one was a tax collector. But what was Judas? We have a few individual stories describing how Jesus met some of the twelve and how he called them while they were fishing or sitting by the customs house collecting the taxes. But when and how did Jesus meet Judas? So many questions about Judas remain wide open. We know one thing for certain, however: Judas was the only Judean among a group of men from the North. Anyone who has ever been an outsider knows what that means. It is difficult to be and feel accepted by a group of people belonging to another race, culture or language. We thus can raise a relevant question: How did the eleven welcome Judas, and how did Judas feel accepted? Remember that Jesus himself, being from Nazareth, was also from Galilee.

Finally, all three gospels have another common element. After Judas' double name, they all add: "the man who was to betray him." The reader just opens the gospels and already the fate of Judas is determined. The name, the place and the qualification for Judas are common to the three synoptic gospels. They also have something else in common. They all place "Simon" first in the list and they all add "to whom he gave the name Peter." The difference is rather remarkable. From the beginning, the reader is told that the one who is always put in first position will receive a new name, and the story will later show the significance of this. But we may at least wonder why Simon Peter is not qualified each time by "the one who would deny him" as Judas is "the one who would betray him." Why always Judas and never Peter?

JUDAS: A Failed Apostle

These texts that speak of the election and mission of the Twelve reveal something to the attentive reader about the great qualities of Judas. The texts may try to hide it by adding "the traitor," but Judas, like all the others, was chosen by Jesus one day. He must have had the qualities required for the task Jesus had in store for them. Like all the others, Judas must have left something behind to follow Jesus. He knew that his acceptance of this challenge would not lead him to a high position humanly speaking, and that this type of life would have its hardships. He had responded to Jesus' call freely; he must have been captivated by Jesus' preaching and way of life. Like all the others, he was sent on a mission (Mark 6:7-13), and when he met up with the others again he must have shared their enthusiasm about the things that had happened during their first pastoral experience: "The apostles rejoined Jesus and told him all they had done and taught" (Mark 6:30). It is important to stress this very positive side of Judas, which has nearly disappeared from the gospels and which we can reconstruct only with some probability. We have stressed before that nobody is only bad or only good; in all of us there is that mixture. Judas too has his beautiful side, even if from the beginning the text tries to hide this by saying, "the man who was to betray him," something that would happen a few years later.

This first text, common to the three synoptic gospels, suggests that Judas was not the one in the group who was put first or who had special privileges. He was the only Judean of the group. He never reappears in a particular gospel story where he would have had a place of honour or special attention. In the gospels some apostles are mentioned by name on a particular occasion. We read how Jesus calls personally Simon and his brother Andrew, James and his brother John (Mark 1:16-20; Luke 5:1-11), and Levi (Luke 5:27-28). John also describes in detail the call of the first disciples: Andrew, Simon, Philip and Nathanael

(John 1:35-51). At the transfiguration, Jesus takes with him Peter, James and John (Matthew 17:1-8). When Jesus gives his eschatological discourse, Peter, James, John and Andrew are mentioned (Mark 13:3). John is even called "the disciple Jesus loved" (John 13:23). Judas is never part of such special events. He never gets a privileged position. This could suggest that Judas was indeed the last on the list, and that he was not really accepted like the others or by the others.

The Gospel of John does not include such a list of the Twelve as the three synoptics do, but very early in that gospel we find a surprising text. After Jesus' discourse on the bread of life, "many of his disciples left him and stopped going with him" (John 6:66). The text continues, "Then Jesus said to the Twelve: 'What about you, do you want to go away too?'" (6:67). No one goes away, which means that Judas remains faithful to Jesus' rather disturbing words. Then follows Peter's profession of faith. He speaks in the plural, and thus in the name of the Twelve: "Lord, who shall we go to? You have the message of eternal life…" (vv. 68-69). To that Jesus replies, "Have I not chosen you Twelve? Yet one of you is a devil" (v. 70). The narrator explains, "He meant Judas son of Simon Iscariot, since this was the man, one of the Twelve, who was going to betray him" (v. 71). Did Jesus say this, or did the gospel writer say he said it? If Jesus did, then Judas was from the beginning stigmatized as a traitor. He must have felt himself an outsider, and been considered one by the others. Whatever happened historically, the text reconfirms for us readers that the name Judas can never appear without the qualification of "traitor."

The next important event in the life of Judas is connected with the anointing at Bethany. The story is told in three gospels but the differences and changes among them are amazing. Jesus is received at Bethany, and during the dinner a woman brings some costly ointment and pours it over Jesus' head. Then follows the reaction: "Some who were there said to one another indignantly, 'Why this waste of ointment? Ointment like this could have been sold for over three hundred denarii and the money given to the poor,' and they were angry with her." (Mark 14:3-9). In the Gospel of Mark, "some who were there" do the complaining. The same story is found in the Gospel of Matthew (Matthew 26:6-13), but now the text says, "When they saw this, the disciples were indignant." And thus, those who do the complaining are no longer "some who were there" but "the disciples."

That story, found in two of the synoptic gospels with no reference to Judas whatsoever, unless indirectly as one of the disciples, is very different in the Gospel of John (John 12:1-11).[14] I will limit myself to indicating only the differences that affect the person of Judas. He appears suddenly in the story and plays an important role in this event. The "some who were there" (Mark), who became "the disciples" (Matthew), now change and become very specific: "Then Judas Iscariot – one of the disciples, the man who was to betray him – said, 'Why wasn't this ointment sold for three hundred denarii, and the money given to the poor?'" (vv. 4-5). Judas' observation is exactly the same as the one attributed to "some" or to "the disciples." In John only, one of the disciples has objections, and it is Judas. And the readers, in case they have forgotten, are reminded once more that he will betray Jesus, a remark that of course has nothing to do with the present story.

In these two synoptic gospels, the "some" or "the disciples" are only indignant and they apparently think about the poor, but nothing else is said about their criticism. John, on the other hand, develops the reason why Judas objects. "He said this, not because he cared about the poor, but because he was a thief; he was in charge of the common fund and used to help himself to the contributions" (v. 6). This verse deserves special attention, because it says several important things about Judas. We are informed that Judas was the bursar of the group. He was in charge of the finances of Jesus and the Twelve. Why was he selected for that position? It would be very enlightening to know precisely why. But since that is not stated, we can only guess. It may indicate that Judas had special talents for that task. Perhaps he was a businessman before Jesus called him. Or maybe he was entrusted with that job to give him some responsibility in the group or even to make him feel valued or useful in that group of all Galileans. Even if we accept that the others had given Judas this job with the best of intentions, we still know one thing for certain; that role in a group is not an easy one. Anyone who has taken on the job of bursar or treasurer knows that this task is extremely delicate; it is very difficult, if not impossible, to please everyone. That job could have increased the rivalry between Judas and the group, as well as the distance between them, leaving Judas even more isolated.

This text touches for the first time on money in the life of Judas. It is going to play a central role in making Judas a traitor. Here the text calls him a "thief" and adds that he used to help himself to the contributions. Money is dangerous; it can become a temptation and it is possible that Judas helped himself occasionally. But at the same time, this information is surprising. Judas, like all the others, must have had a job before he accepted Jesus' call. He had given it up to follow Jesus, knowing that he was not going to become rich in doing so. This suggests that Judas had shown himself to be detached from money and wealth. We can also ask how the others knew that Judas was a "thief," as John calls him. If they knew that he helped himself to the contributions, why did they keep him in charge of the common fund? Why did they not give that position to another member of the group instead? After all, there was also a tax collector among them who knew how to manage money. He could have taken over from Judas.

JUDAS: A Failed Apostle

Even stating that Judas was a thief has nothing to do with the present story and with Judas' words. All he said was that all the money the woman spent on the ointment should have been given to the poor. He never suggested that this money should have been put into the common fund, in the hope that he could then take some of it for himself. The narrator seems to twist the story. He says first of all that Judas did not care about the poor. He does not take Judas' words seriously. That Judas said explicitly that the money should have gone to the poor indicates that he cared for the poor, just like the "some" or "the disciples" in the synoptics who said the same thing. Second, the narrator adds that Judas is a thief. But how could Judas have stolen the money for the ointment if it were given to the poor? The only thing this text accomplishes is to show once more a lack of respect for Judas.

Another event in the life of Judas mentioned in the three synoptic gospels is how Judas offers to hand Jesus over to the Jewish authorities. "Judas Iscariot, one of the Twelve, approached the chief priests with an offer to hand Jesus over to them. They were delighted to hear it, and promised to give him money; and he looked for a way of betraying him when the opportunity should occur" (Mark 14:10-11). The text does not explain how Judas came to this point in his life or outline his motivations. The authorities are delighted; they offer him some money and the deal is done. Now it is a question of finding the right moment to betray Jesus. This is a simple version of the event; Luke presents it in a slightly different form (Luke 22:3-6), explaining how Judas came to this terrible decision: "Then Satan entered into Judas, surnamed Iscariot" (v. 3). This statement resembles what is said in the story of Saul: "Now the spirit of the LORD had left Saul and an evil spirit from the LORD filled him…" (1 Samuel 16:14). It seems almost impossible to comprehend why one of the Twelve would offer to betray Jesus. Since this action is so mysterious, it is attributed to an outside power entering Judas. Satan is the personification of evil; evil has taken over. But then the question is this: Why did Satan enter into Judas and not another person? Satan or evil can so overpower a person that this person can be identified as Satan, as Jesus once said to Peter: "Get behind me, Satan!" (Matthew 16:23). According to Luke, the priests and Judas discussed a scheme for handing Jesus over. The authorities also agreed to give Judas some money.

Matthew describes that same event very differently (Matthew 26:14-15). When Judas goes to see the chief priests, he says: "What are you prepared to give me if I hand him over to you?" This time the reason for Judas' betrayal is explained in clear terms; Judas is looking for money. That seems to be his main preoccupation. Matthew thus makes money very important in the life of Judas, as John did for the anointing at Bethany. In the texts of Mark and Luke, the priests promised to give Judas some money, but according to Matthew, "They paid him thirty silver pieces." They don't just promise, they give him the money right away. Even the amount is specified: it corresponds to the price the law fixed for the life of a slave (Exodus 21:32). The money that was supposed to be compensation for the betrayal has become the motive for the betrayal. Judas is looking to enrich himself. The betrayal is presented as a business transaction.

The next event in the life of Judas happens at the Last Supper, when Jesus foretells Judas' treachery. All the gospels include this story. Mark's report is sober (Mark 14:17-21). "And while they were at table eating, Jesus said, 'I tell you solemnly, one of you is about to betray me, one of you eating with me.'" We can only guess how this must have shocked the Twelve. Their reaction is understandable: "They were distressed and asked him, one after another, 'Not I, surely?'" Each raises this question one after the other, which means that Judas, too, must have asked it. It is of course difficult to read into his heart and understand how he could even say it. Jesus' response remains general; he does not name the person in question: "It is one of the Twelve, one who is dipping into the same dish with me. Yes, the Son of Man is going to his fate, as the scriptures say he will, but alas for that man by whom the Son of Man is betrayed! Better for that man if he had never been born." Jesus indicates that what is going to happen to him belongs to his fate, belongs to God's plan as stipulated in the Scriptures, but that it is at the same time the work of Judas. Judas is thus part of God's plan, so does he choose freely to betray Jesus? Even when Satan took him over, was Judas free? The scene in Mark is discreet. None of the others know who the betrayer is – only Jesus and Judas. How did Judas feel, especially after hearing the hard words that it would be better that he had never been born?

This same event is reported even more soberly by Luke, but there are some differences (Luke 22:21-23). Jesus declares that he goes "to his fate even as it has been decreed." Here Jesus stresses even more strongly than in Mark that everything that will happen to him has been predetermined. The Twelve here do not ask Jesus who could be the traitor, and so Judas escapes asking the question "Not I, surely?" – a question that in his mouth is rather sarcastic. According to Luke, the Twelve "began to ask one another which of them it could be who was to do this thing." In such a conversation, Judas could remain very quiet without becoming hypocritical.

As we have seen, Matthew gives a more explicit report of Judas' offer to hand Jesus over. He makes things worse in this encounter at the Last Supper (Matthew 26:20-25). The text is very similar to the Mark's, and it follows the same structure. Jesus announces that one of the Twelve will betray him, the disciples ask who it could be, Jesus replies and adds that it would have been better for that man never to have been born. The text apparently has come to an end, but suddenly continues. What happens next seems out of place, since the disciples had already asked who it could be. Now "Judas, who was to betray him, asked in his turn, 'Not I, Rabbi, surely?'" (v. 25a). The text concentrates on Judas, who is now presented very strongly as a hypocrite, which was much less obvious in the two other synoptic gospels. Jesus answers Judas directly: "They are your own words" (v. 25b). If that is how the event went historically, then all the Twelve knew without a doubt that Judas would be the traitor. But we hear no comment by anyone; none of the Twelve make the slightest effort to talk him out of carrying out his project.

This scene of the Last Supper is even more developed in John's gospel (John 13). Right at the beginning of that long story we find a reference to Judas: "They were at supper, and the devil had already put it into the mind of Judas Iscariot son of Simon, to betray him" (v. 2). Like Luke, who said that Satan had entered into Judas, John says that the devil was at work in Judas. He explains that what is going on in the heart of Judas is evil, personified by the devil. Later, during the meal, Jesus foretells the treachery of Judas (vv. 21-30). This report, which is the most developed of all the gospels, provides new elements that can help us understand Judas better. After Jesus tells his disciples that one of them will betray him, "the disciples looked at one another, wondering which he meant" (v. 22). They do not ask Jesus anything more, or discuss it among themselves. Here the story is totally different. "The disciple Jesus loved was reclining next to Jesus; Simon Peter signed to him and said, 'Ask who it is he means.' So leaning back on Jesus' breast he said, 'Who is it, Lord?'" (vv. 23-25). The scene illustrates that some of the Twelve had better places at table than others, and Judas was not one of the favoured ones. This brings us back to the question of how Judas was welcomed into this group of Galileans. The conversation appears to be rather private between John and Jesus. Jesus answers, "It is the one to whom I give the piece of bread that I shall dip in the dish" (v. 26a) and immediately "he dipped the piece of bread and gave it to Judas son of Simon Iscariot" (v. 26b). This is a clear answer, and so is Jesus' action. If, as the texts suggest, this conversation was not heard by everybody at the table, that implies that only John knew the answer, and may have shared it with Peter. What follows seems to confirm that the others were not aware of what was going on.

After Judas took the piece of bread, the text adds, "Satan entered him" (v. 27a), reinforcing what was said in the beginning of the story: that the devil was already in the mind of Judas. And now Jesus addresses himself to Judas directly: "What you are going to do, do quickly" (v. 27b). This is a very strange order. What if Jesus had said, "Why would you do this? Stay with us." The others do not know what he means: "None of the others at table understood the reason he said this" (v. 28). They obviously must not have heard that Judas was going to betray him. They interpret Jesus' words in their own way: "Since Judas had charge of the common fund, some of them thought Jesus was telling him, 'Buy what we need for the festival,' or telling him to give something to the poor"(v. 29). John had mentioned at the occasion of the anointing at Bethany that Judas was in charge of the common fund; he repeats here that Judas was the bursar of the group. But now we read, to our surprise, that Judas was such a generous man that he would be ready to leave a party to look after the poor. That is different from what was said about him in the Bethany story, where he was accused of not caring at all about the poor.

That story of the Last Supper ends with these words: "As soon as Judas had taken the piece of bread he went out" (v. 30). That is a rather strange and unexpected ending. Those attending a party with friends do not like to see someone leave early. They would ask that person to stay, or at least ask why he has to go so soon. Why did no one ask

Judas where he had to go? Why did no one press him to stay? It does not make much sense to believe that someone would leave a party just to go and give something to the poor. Is the errand urgent? Could it not wait for another hour or so? Nobody seems to regret that Judas leaves. What does that say about them? And even if Judas had to go to buy something, like some of them thought, why did they not wonder why he did not come back after a while? There seems to be no sign of that kind of simple, good human relationship that we expect to see in a group of friends. Does this prove that Judas was never really accepted, and that he always must have felt left out? This lack of interest in Judas becomes even more depressing if we compare it with a question that Jesus asks his disciples in his farewell discourse during that same supper. Jesus speaks about his departure, mentioning that he is going to the one who sent him. Then he says to his disciples, "Not one of you has asked, 'Where are you going?'" (John 16:5). Neither did anyone ask Judas, "Where are you going?" We cannot help but wonder if things would have been different if they had done so.

Later, but still at the Last Supper, Jesus, in what is called his priestly prayer, speaks about the disciples and makes another reference to Judas: "I have watched over them and not one is lost except the one who chose to be lost, and this was to fulfill the scriptures" (John 17:12). This statement is very cryptic. When Jesus says that he watched over them, does he include Judas in the group? If he does, how did Judas become lost? The text provides a double answer. On the one hand, Judas made that choice, but on the other hand it happened to fulfill the Scriptures; it is thus part of God's plan. How can it be both a free choice by Judas and something that is predetermined by God? This situation resembles the fate of Saul.

The next event in the life of Judas is Jesus' arrest in the garden of Gethsemane. All four gospels describe this

encounter. We start once again from the description of
the arrest given by Mark (Mark 14:43-47). "Judas, one of
the Twelve, came up with a number of men armed with
swords and clubs…" (v. 43). Judas appears as the leader of
the group, or as the guide who brings these armed men to
Jesus. "Now the traitor had arranged a signal with them:
'The one I kiss'…. So when the traitor came he went
straight up to Jesus and said, 'Rabbi!' and kissed him" (vv.
44-45). The text repeats twice the word "traitor," stressing
Judas' action. He betrays Jesus with a kiss, a fact that is
also mentioned twice. Judas says only one word to Jesus
– "Rabbi!" Jesus does not say anything to him.

Luke, in his description of the arrest, is very sober
(Luke 22:47-51). The word "traitor" does not appear in
the text. Judas does not say a word, but now Jesus speaks
to him: "Judas, are you betraying the Son of Man with a
kiss?" (v. 48). Jesus addresses him by his personal name,
surely a sign of some intimacy. But how do we have to
understand this question of Jesus? Is it a final invitation to
Judas to change his mind, or is it a reproach, an accusation?
Whatever it may be, this question must have made Judas
feel more guilty.

The story is again slightly different in the Gospel of
Matthew (Matthew 26:47-50). The word "traitor" appears
once. Judas says to Jesus: "Greetings, Rabbi," and Jesus
replies, "My friend, do what you are here for" (v. 50). This
statement is not too clear, and can also be interpreted as a
question or reproach. It is interesting, however, to note the
title Jesus uses to address Judas: "friend." Does that term
hint at a last chance for Judas, or is it deep sarcasm: you as
a friend do such things? Judas must feel even more guilty,
hearing Jesus call him "friend."

The Gospel of John gives a report of Jesus' arrest that
is very different from that of the synoptic gospels (John
18:1-9). The text twice refers to "Judas the traitor." Judas'
name is linked to what he does; he is no longer called

"one of the Twelve," or simply "Judas" or "friend." There is no reference to Judas kissing Jesus; the text says only that Judas knew where Jesus was, that he brought the cohort to that place and that he was standing among them. Judas does not say anything to Jesus, and Jesus says nothing to him. But the text of John stresses very strongly something else: "Knowing everything that was going to happen to him" (v. 4) and also "This was to fulfill the words he had spoken…" (v. 9). We are once more faced with that hidden divine plan, that fate and consequently the question about Judas' freedom.

The last event of the Judas story is his tragic death. Only the Gospel of Matthew gives this information (Matthew 27:3-10). It is important to note where Matthew places this text. It follows soon after Jesus' arrest, in which Judas played an important role (26:47-56). Jesus is then taken to Caiaphas, the high priest, where he is accused of blasphemy (26:57-68). While that session is going on, Peter denies Jesus in the courtyard. (26:69-75). It is decided to bring Jesus to Pilate (27:1-2). Then the story returns to Judas: "When he found that Jesus had been condemned, Judas his betrayer was filled with remorse" (v. 3a). Judas' reaction is not after Jesus' death, but after Jesus is condemned. Judas may have expected this to happen, but at this point he cannot be sure that Jesus will be put to death.

And yet, even Jesus' condemnation moves Judas deeply. This is the first time that we can see into the heart of Judas, and what we find there is something very positive and moving; he is "filled with remorse." This is the first time a gospel says something positive about Judas, but it still adds, as always, that negative note: "his betrayer." But Judas does not merely feel remorse. He also wants to make amends. "He took the thirty silver pieces back to the chief priests and elders" (v. 3b). He does not want to keep that money he had asked for and received as a condition for handing

Jesus over to them (if we follow how it is presented only in the same Gospel of Matthew; 26:14-16).

Judas uses profound words: "I have sinned; I have betrayed innocent blood" (v. 4a). He recognizes, not only in his heart but openly to the priests, that he has sinned; he has the courage to admit that he did something wrong. Not all sinners are ready to admit this! These words remind us of Saul, who also confessed his sins first to Samuel (1 Samuel 15:24) and later to David (1 Samuel 26:17). Judas must have hoped that his confession would have an impact on the priests and that they might stop Jesus' trial. But Judas encounters only rejection:"'What is that to us?' they replied. 'That is your concern'" (v. 4b). We notice again the parallel with the Saul story: after confessing his sins, he too begged for some understanding. He asked Samuel and David to come back with him, but both refused. What would Saul's story have been if he had encountered understanding? Judas, who is filled with remorse and who openly confesses his sins, is also faced with refusal. The priests show him complete indifference, making no effort to listen to him.

Judas is rejected by those he had hoped to serve. He knows he will no longer be welcome in the group of the Twelve, who perhaps had never really accepted him and who only saw him as the traitor. Peter, after his denial of Jesus, got another chance when "the Lord turned and looked straight at Peter" (Luke 22:61), but Judas never saw Jesus again; he did not have Peter's privilege. So what are Judas's options? We know nothing about his family in Kerioth – would they welcome him in now? He himself does not see any way out. He is the big loser, the failed apostle. The text then summarizes in three short actions what he considers the only solution (v. 5). "And flinging down the silver pieces in the sanctuary" – Judas had offered to return the money to the priests, but they have refused. The only place where that dirty money might still be turned to a positive use is the sanctuary, to pay for some sacrifices offered to God or to help the poor. At least Judas is now free of the burden of caring about money, which had been his job for these past few years with the Twelve. Then "he made off and went."

Judas leaves the sanctuary all alone, without any friends, and then "he hanged himself." Judas takes his own life out of despair. Once again he resembles Saul, who also ended his life by self-killing to save his honour; and also Samson. For both of these men, at least some people cared about them and made sure they had a decent funeral. But no one cares about Judas. When someone commits suicide, family and friends generally ask themselves the same anguished, soul-searching questions: What did we do that he or she came to this desperate act? How could we have prevented this? Did he or she perhaps not feel accepted? It does not appear, at least in the text, that anyone ever asked such questions about Judas.

The text about Judas ends with "he hanged himself." It is as if he is still hanging there – no funeral, no grave, nothing. The story seems to be more concerned about the money, because that is what is discussed further. The priests pick up the money and they say: "It is against the Law to put this into the treasury; it is blood-money" (v. 6). In a sense, this is a final insult to Judas. He had hoped that the money could have served in the sanctuary, but even that is not acceptable. So they "bought the potter's field with it as a graveyard for foreigners" (v. 7). At least the money had some use, for dead foreigners, people whom Judas may have understood better than the other Twelve, since he himself was a foreigner among them. The field was called "Field of Blood" – in Aramaic, "Hakeldama." The story ends by saying that in this way "the words of the prophet Jeremiah were then fulfilled" (v. 9). Once again we touch on that mystery of fate and of God's plan in what Judas did.

Only the Gospel of Matthew gives us a report of Judas' death. But Luke refers to it in his second book, the Acts of the Apostles (Acts 1:15-20). There he presents Peter's speech when Matthias is elected to replace Judas: "One day Peter stood up to speak to the brothers.... The passage of Scripture had to be fulfilled in which the Holy Spirit, speaking through David, foretells the fate of Judas" (v. 16a). He also refers a few other times to biblical texts (v. 20). We thus hear once more about that "fate" of Judas; what he did was to fulfill the Scriptures! Judas' actions are predetermined by God's plan. Peter summarizes a few important events in the life of Judas. He begins with the negative – the bad thing Judas did towards the end: "who offered himself as guide to the men who arrested Jesus" (v. 16b).

This is perhaps the first time, however, outside of the gospels that Judas is not stigmatized as "the traitor"; he has served as "guide." But Peter also mentions explicitly the good side of Judas: "after having been one of our numbers and actually sharing this ministry of ours" (v. 17). One only wonders why Peter did not start with that, for Judas indeed shared that ministry first, and for a few years. In any case, Peter admits that everything in Judas' life has not been bad. Peter then moves to the last events in Judas' life. "He bought a field with the money he was paid for his crime" (v. 18a). This is completely different from Matthew's version. According to Luke, not the priests but Judas himself bought that field. In Luke's version, he kept the money and invested it in a piece of land for his own use. And Peter goes on: "He fell headlong and burst open, and all his entrails poured out" (v. 18b). What a gruesome description. Who would describe the death of a friend or relative in such terms? And of course we wonder: Did Judas hang himself or not? How did he fall and why? Once more we notice a similarity with the Saul story: Saul's death, too, was reported in two conflicting versions. Even in his death Judas is abused! Peter then says, "Everybody in Jerusalem heard about it" (v. 19). But why, then, did no one care for the dead body and look after Judas' funeral and burial? Peter affirms that the field that Judas bought with his money was called "the Bloody Acre," or in Aramaic, "Hakeldama," perhaps because of the blood of Judas, who burst open in that field. This also differs from Matthew, who says that it was called "Bloody Field" because it was bought with the money that Judas got to betray innocent blood of Jesus.

Theological Conclusion

We do not have the full life story of the apostle Judas. He is mentioned only in a few texts in the gospels: the list of the Twelve, the anointing at Bethany, his offer to betray Jesus, his presence at the Last Supper, his role in the arrest of Jesus, and his death. This, of course, is not enough to give a complete picture of this person whose life was such a tragedy.

All of these texts are clearly written from a very negative view of Judas by people who were supposed to be his friends. There is certainly no tendency to place his actions in a good light or to find excuses for what he did. On the contrary, he is continually blamed and identified with one single thing he did in his life. Whatever else he may have done, good or bad, disappears under the title "the traitor." The stories in the various gospels are often so different, and at times are even contrary to each other, that it is impossible even to guess which version is closer to what happened historically. But still, using what we have and taking the texts for what they are, we can say a few things about Judas.

Judas must have been a very fine person. Jesus obviously had good reasons to choose him to become one of the Twelve. Judas, like the others, accepted his call and did his ministry for several years. After Jesus' discourse on the bread of life, which was disturbing, many of his disciples left, while Judas stayed faithfully with Jesus. There must thus have been something loveable about him, since Jesus calls him "friend." The biblical text also admits that he was a sincere person with a great heart who could be filled with remorse. He regretted what he did. He was also an honest person with the courage to say publicly, "I have sinned." He did not try to find excuses, or to blame the priests, the other apostles or anyone else. He just said: I did it!

Nobody is totally good or totally bad. Judas, like all human beings, had his weak points. It is clear and affirmed in all four gospels that Judas betrayed Jesus. It is obviously a very sad thing to betray the person who had called him and shown him full confidence. To betray a person is seen in all cultures as something repulsive. But how Judas came to this point is far from clear. Some of the texts insist that he was too attached to money, and even that he was a thief. They thus suggest that this motive may have led him to betray Jesus. Human history is full of such cases: people are capable of doing terrible things just for the money. As we saw earlier, Delilah betrayed Samson for big money. But we still may wonder if Judas' love of money was truly what led him to betray Jesus. When he agreed to follow Jesus, he must have given up his job, whatever that was. He must have known that there was not much chance for him to become rich by following Jesus. That suggests that he was detached from money, but it does not necessarily rule out his becoming greedy later.

But not all texts suggest that money was the reason for his betrayal of Jesus. We can then only guess at what may have been the deep reason for such a change in the life of Judas, from disciple to traitor. All leaders have a support group: political leaders and also spiritual leaders, such as the prophets. Jesus had his support group, and Judas was part of it. But members of such support groups may leave their leader for all kinds of reasons, especially out of disappointment with the leader. It may be that Judas became disappointed in Jesus: in his person, in his ministry, in his preaching, in his behaviour, or some other dimension. This of course does not justify Judas' betrayal of Jesus as leader. Judas could have opted simply to quit the group.

But two points deserve special attention in the Judas story. First, how was Judas accepted by the group? And, linked with that question, to what extent does the group share some responsibility for what Judas did? Judas was the only Judean in a group of Galileans; he may have felt less accepted. Even though the others may have given him responsibility over the common fund, this could have increased the frictions between them. At the Last Supper, they never tried to change his mind; they never invited him or begged him to stay with the group. According to the gospels, they do not show much respect for Judas. Could it be that they, too, have some responsibility for what happened? We have compared Saul's story with Judas' several times. We wondered if Saul's life could have turned out differently if Samuel and David had responded to him. In the same way, if the group had acted differently, would Judas have betrayed Jesus?

Second, we must consider the frequent references to "fate," to that mysterious divine plan. The gospels say several times that all Judas did was in order to fulfill what was written in the Scriptures. At times, the text also says that Satan entered into Judas – another similarity with Saul's story. And so the Judas story raises the same theological questions as the Saul story: Who is the God of this story? Judas is responsible for his actions, but at the same time his life seems to be predetermined by God or by fate. Again we see the mysterious dark side of God, found in the Old and New Testaments, and are left with unanswered questions.

Conclusion

Some people expect, when they open the Bible, to find stories about saints or people whose life is an example to be imitated. The five stories of biblical human failures that we have presented are the best proof that this is not the case. On the contrary, the Bible presents real people, and no one is totally perfect or totally bad. At times, the Bible describes the life of people whose good side seems to be dominant; in this book, I have chosen people whose evil side has led them to failure. I have taken people from the Old and from the New Testament, covering different periods of the history of Israel and highlighting people who played different but important roles in that history: Lot, the failed patriarch; Samson, the failed judge; Saul, the failed king; Jonah, the failed prophet; and Judas, the failed apostle.

All five are losers – people who did not make it in the role they were called to play. Their stories are, of course, written by the winners and are thus presented from that perspective. The historical value of the reports varies from story to story, but they all have the same intention: to entertain and to teach. That these stories entertain does not mean that they invite the reader to laugh. The reader may laugh while reading the story of Jonah in the belly of the fish, but such a response shows that the person's reading is superficial, and that he or she has missed the point. We would wonder at a reader who enjoyed the Samson story. These five stories make us rather feel sad and even angry about some stupid and tragic human behaviour. At the same time, they create in us some pity and even sympathy for the way these people ruined any chance of success for themselves. For several of them, success seemed to be within their reach, while for others, their fight seemed hopeless, doomed by some hidden, predetermined fate. These five stories teach us something profound about life and death.

If we look at these figures and what they did with their lives, we see some good in each one of them – something that, had it been more developed, could have prevented failure. At the same time, we see their weaknesses. Lot was a good person. He could be very generous, but he was a kind of unbeliever, and when he had the chance he wanted to make his own decisions about his life. The disappointments he felt about the choices he made rendered him unable to make any more decisions. Samson was deeply loved by his exemplary parents, who gave him the best possible education. He received from them all he needed to make something beautiful of his life and of his mission at the service of his people. But he had no social conscience or concern for his people. He showed no interest in looking after their well-being. Instead, he preferred to be a womanizer. And perhaps to impress these attractive women he made big shows of his extraordinary strength, to the point of becoming cruel, unjust and violent to the extreme. Saul was a young man who had all the qualities required to become the first king of Israel, and to be a successful one. And indeed, that is how people saw and respected him for a long time. But this all changed when he saw the popularity of David, whom he dearly loved, eclipse his own. Saul became jealous, and fear of losing his authority spoiled the rest of his life. He became obsessed by that fear, seeing conspiracy everywhere. That fear led him to self-pity, and from there to anger, hatred and violence. Jonah also had his good qualities. He was ready to sacrifice his own life to save the sailors in the storm. He must have been a good speaker, since after only one day of preaching, the sinful people of Nineveh converted. But Jonah was at the same time a very narrow-minded person, closed to God and to others, full of self-pity and anger. He was deeply unhappy, with no joy in his own life, and unable to rejoice in the happiness of others. Judas, who was an apostle for a few years, a member of the Twelve, could only have been successful in this venture because of his personal qualities. He was a person with deep feelings and could be very honest, but money may have made him greedy. Disappointment in Jesus and perhaps the lack of feeling accepted by the others may have coloured his views.

If we take a closer look at these five men, we notice that their lives and thus their failures were caused not only by what they were and did themselves, but also by some people with whom they lived. Lot frequently was not free to make his own decisions. Others did it for him: Terah his grandfather; Abraham his uncle; and above all his daughters, who abused their father scandalously. Samson used women, but he was also abused by some of them, who betrayed him for money. While he took revenge on people, they were not ready to forgive. They also practised violence and thus incited Samson to more of the same. The attitude of so many people towards Saul affected him deeply, to the point of changing him completely. His son and daughter showed more loyalty to David than to their own father, as did several other important religious, political and military leaders. Above all, the refusal Saul got from Samuel and David even after expressing clearly his regret, raises serious questions about their responsibility for what happened to him. Jonah seemed to be a loner. No one else appeared to have much impact on him. For Judas, the question of the role the others played in his life is a serious one. He is always presented as the scapegoat in the group; they did not seem to try to help him to change his mind.

Finally, in the lives of these men, there is also God. God is at work in the life of Lot, and appears to be on his side in several instances. He makes sure that Lot and his family can be saved, and each time he accepts Lot's request for where he wants to go. In the life of Samson we see several references to the spirit of God descending on him. But that makes him able to do strange things; thanks to that divine spirit, Samson is capable of killing many Philistines. Does that God only care about Samson, and not about the victims of his brutality? The God in the life of Saul becomes even more problematic. He chooses Saul to be the king and then drops him totally; not only does the spirit of God leave Saul, but an evil spirit takes over. We have suggested that the Saul story illustrates that dark side of God. Why is he against Saul but with David? In the Jonah story God comes out as a more sympathetic player. He not only cares about his prophet Jonah, he is also deeply concerned about the people of Nineveh. For Judas, the mysterious God reappears. Satan simply takes over the mind and heart of Judas. The bad thing Judas did was all part of a predetermined divine plan, as predicted in the Scriptures, at times in detail.

These failed characters made their mistakes. They did not control themselves as they should have. But others played a role in their failure, too. And there is that open question about the mysterious place of God in their lives, for which we try to find an answer.

These men became failures sooner or later during their lives, but what is even more depressing is that they were also failures in their deaths. Two of them may have died what we would call a natural death, but even these are somewhat tragic. Lot ends his life hiding in a cave, a place where the dead are kept; there he stays, still alive, in darkness and in fear. In a sense there is no life for him anymore; he already seems to sojourn in sheol. Jonah nearly disappears in the sea and is swallowed by a fish – what he himself describes as being in sheol. Any other normal person, after such an experience, would cling to his life as long as possible; not Jonah. Some of his last words are a prayer begging God to let him die. He prefers death to life: failed life, failed death.

For Saul and for Judas, we have two different descriptions of their last days, but for both of them one account speaks of self-killing. If we follow these texts, then three of the five failed characters died in this tragic way. Suicide is very rare in the Bible, but all too common in our world. Some see in it a positive, honourable deed; others condemn it as sin, as a sign of madness or of social disintegration. Samson, Saul and Judas too acted for different reasons. Samson may appear to be a kind of suicide bomber: by offering his own life, he kills thousands of the enemy, perhaps to the joy of his own people. But his deed is not all that "pure"; he committed suicide to kill but also because he himself could not live any longer with his miserable condition of being blind and in an enemy prison. King Saul committed suicide to save his own honour; he did not want to fall into the hands of the enemy. Judas took his own life apparently out of despair. He felt rejected by everyone; he had no place to go – and that is the reason for so many suicides in our day. For Samson and for Saul there was at least some closure. Family or friends cared about them, took the body and provided them with a funeral and a burial place. Judas did not even get this much.

Five sad stories, five ruined lives, five failed people. What can we learn from them? These stories invite us to avoid failure in our lives – to strive to make our lives success stories. These biblical stories also make us aware of the potential within us to make the lives of others failures or successes. These five stories, therefore, play an important role in the Bible and deserve their place in the canon.

Notes

1 Walter Vogels, *Nos Origines*: Genèse 1–11, Montréal, Fides, 2000 (2ᵉ Ed.).

2 Walter Vogels, "Sara: Een mooie vrouw" in *Vrouwen in het Oude Testament*, Leuven, Vlaamse Bijbelstichting; 's Hertogenbosch, Katholieke Bijbelstichting, 1993, pp. 21–17.

3 Walter Vogels, "'Osée - Gomer' car et comme 'Yahweh – Israel': Osée 1–3" *Nouvelle revue théologique*, 103 (1981), pp. 711–727; id., "Diachronic and Synchronic Studies of Hosea 1–3", *Biblische Zeitschrift*, 28 (1984), pp. 94–98.

4 W.Vogels, *Abraham et sa légende*: Genese 12,1–25,11 (Lire la Bible 110), Paris Cerf; Montréal, Médiaspaul, 1996; id., *Moise aux multiples visages*: De L'Exode au Deuteronome (Lire la Bible 114), Paris, Cerf; Montréal, Médiaspaul, 1997; id., *David et son histoire*: 1 Samuel 16,1 – 1 Rois 2,11, Montréal, Médiaspaul, 2003.

5 Walter Vogels, "Hagar: De draagmoeder", in *Vrouwen in het Oude Testament*, Leuven, Vlaamse Bijbelstichting; 's Hertogenbosch, Katholieke Bijbelstichting, 1993, pp. 29–34.

6 See some of my previous studies on Lot: Walter Vogels, "Abraham et l'offrande de la terre (Gen 13)," *Studies in Religion / Sciences religieuses* 4 (1974), pp. 51–57; id., "Lot, père des incroyants," *Église et Théologie*, 6 (1975), pp. 139–151; id., "Lot in His Honor Restored: A Structural Analysis of Gen 13:2-18," *Église et Théologie*, 10 (1979), pp. 5–12, also in *Reading and Preaching the Bible: A New Semiotic Approach* (Background Books 4), Wilmington, DE, Michael Glazier, 1986, pp. 133–148; and also my book on Abraham, in which I analyze all the texts related to Lot, *Abraham et sa légende*: Genèse 12,1–15,11 (Lire la Bible 110), Paris, Cerf: Montréal, Médiaspaul, 1996.

7 In the beginning of the Abraham-cycle the hero is always called Abram; that name will be changed to Abraham by God (17:5). In this book I will, however, use the best-known name Abraham right from the beginning. The same applies to Sarai, who becomes Sarah (17:15).

8 In this book, following the practice of most modern biblical translations, we have replaced the name "Yahweh" with "the Lᴏʀᴅ". To avoid profaning the sacred name, in their reading Jewish people would substitute *adonai* ("my Lord") for the written "Yahweh." "The Lᴏʀᴅ" (with capital letters) thus refers to

171

the divine, and is distinct from "lord" (in lower case), which refers to a human being.

9   Walter Vogels, "Hospitality in Biblical Perspective," *Liturgical Ministry*, 11 (2002), pp. 162–173.

10   Walter Vogels, *Samson: Sexe – Violence – Religion*, Coll. Écritures 10, Bruxelles, Lumen Vitae; Ottawa, Novalis, 2006.

11   Walter Vogels, *David et son histoire*: 1 Samuel 16,1 – 1 Rois 2,11, Montréal, Médiaspaul, 2003.

12   The biblical texts from now on are centred on Saul and on David. These stories (1 Samuel 16–31) can thus be considered as belonging to the David story since they describe his ascent to the throne, or they can be considered as part of the Saul story, since they describe his downfall. In this study I read them from Saul's perspective, which means that I will not comment on texts that only speak of David. I studied all these chapters in more detail in Walter Vogels, *David et son histoire*: 1 Samuel 16,1 – 1 Rois 2,11, Montréal, Médiaspaul, 2003, pp. 35–154.

13   Walter Vogels, "'Spreken doden nog?' Saul en Samuel in En-Dor," *Jota*, 6 (1994), n.23, pp. 15–23.

14   Walter Vogels, "De la mort à la vie vers la mort: Analyse sémiotique de Jean 12,1-11," in Adèle Chené, Pierrette Daviau et autres, *De Jésus et des femmes*: Lectures sémiotiques, suivies d'une entrevue avec A.Y. Greimas, Coll. Recherches: Nouvelle Série 14, Montréal, Bellarmin; Paris, Cerf, 1987, pp. 157–172.

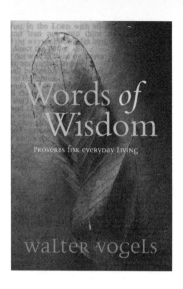

In this lively work, biblical scholar Walter Vogels shows the role that proverbs and aphorisms play in our everyday lives, and relates our experience to the Wisdom tradition in Scripture. Collecting proverbs from a wide array of religions, times and cultures, the author skillfully demonstrates how these spiritual nuggets from both within and outside the biblical tradition help give shape and breadth to our day-to-day experience.

"If the wisdom contained in proverbs must be appropriated anew by each generation, here is an indispensable 'word to the wise' and sage guide for the journey."—*Normand Bonneau, Professor of New Testament, Saint Paul University, Ottawa*

NOVALIS

1-800-387-7164

www.novalis.ca

What is so special about the Bible? Why do people continue to value it 2000 years after Christ? The Bible – the inspired Word of God – expresses real people's experiences and invites us to enter into them. For this reason, the Bible is not simply to be read, but above all to be lived.

Living according to the Bible demands that we be open to God, act in solidarity with others and respect nature. In *Becoming Fully Human,* renowned Scripture scholar Walter Vogels shows how each of us can "live" the Bible by discovering and acting on certain life principles and deep human values that transcend time and culture.

NOVALIS

1-800-387-7164

www.novalis.ca